Praise
The Essential Handb

"This book is clear and easy to read and understand. I read it with the intent to critique and make suggestions on content. I can't find anything to say except 'great job,' again."

Terry Parker
Green Tree Properties

"I LOVE IT!! I appreciate how Karen makes it so easy to read and follow. She walks you through the 'real world' of being a landlord and not only shares the good, but the bad and the reality!"

Veronica Serna
Trust Real Estate Investments

"Regardless of your goal, having the best teacher is essential to success. More importantly, knowing what steps to follow and when to make them are critical. In *The Essential Handbook for Landlords*, the newest installment in Karen's collection of handbooks, she provides needed information with the obvious knowledge of an industry expert. With Karen as your guide, success is inevitable."

Arminda Lindsay

"Karen's guidance has removed a lot of anxiety from the landlording process. As a fairly new investor, dealing with tenants was uncharted territory for me. I now have confidence that I can successfully market and quickly fill properties with *qualified tenants.*"

Jen Wong
Fillmore Properties

The Essential Handbook for Landlords

The Essential Handbook

FOR LANDLORDS

Karen Rittenhouse

Southeastern Investments, LLC
Greensboro, North Carolina

Published by Southeastern Investments, LLC
Greensboro, North Carolina

ISBN 13: 978-0-9837752-2-5
Library of Congress Control Number: 2012915104

First Southeastern Investments, LLC printing: September 2012

Dedication

*To all those providing safe,
affordable housing for others.*

Contents

Section Three: The Paperwork / 67

Acknowledgements

I'd like to thank my many friends, tenants, and homeowners who assisted me as I went through my landlording learning and growing process. Thank you for all the experience you provided throughout my journey.

And, of course I want to acknowledge the three men in my life, my boys John and Glenn, and my husband, Jim, for always being my reason.

Introduction

Why read this book?

Because there is so much wealth to be created from owning real estate. The more you know about how to do it right, the easier and more profitable landlording will be.

This book contains the valuable information I've gained through much work over many years. By passing this on to you, you will profit much faster than I did. The information found here will save you time, help you avoid potential problems, and enable you to make money that you wouldn't make without the knowledge it contains.

So, how can you get on board this phenomenon known as landlording?

Let me assure you, it's absolutely possible and not terribly difficult. How do I know? Because I stumbled in complete ignorance into this world filled with tenants (in many ways, my ignorance was a good thing) and ended up creating a financially secure retirement for my family and myself.

Creating wealth through real estate is not a get rich quick experience. Instead, settle in for a business that will grow over time in both properties and income. I want you to look forward to and enjoy the gradual process of acquiring, fixing up, filling, and managing properties, just as I have.

You will discover how being a landlord can allow you to help others by providing a secure place for them to live, how to manage and run your own business, and how to generate perpetual cash-flow and secure your own retirement. You will learn that allowing others to pay down your mortgage creates the income you need for the future.

As you read, you'll find answers to your questions including: Is this a good time to be a landlord? How do I find a rental property? How do I find a qualified tenant? What if the tenants tear up my house? What paperwork do I need?

I have been involved in real estate investing full-time since January 2005 when I quit my W-2 job and started buying rental properties to secure our retirement. Two years later, we owned twenty-five properties and my husband quit his W-2 job to join me. We currently employ full-time employees, buy and sell multiple properties every month, manage more than 150 homes, and help others to do the same.

In helping others buy, renovate, fill, and manage properties, we find that most landlords express the same questions and concerns. In this book, I'm going to share some of the most frequently discussed questions and answers for people who are, just like you, interested in owning and managing real estate.

If you're considering becoming a landlord, or even if you already are, this book provides tips and insights to make your business easier and more profitable.

As you read, you'll find answers to your questions including: Is this a good time to be a landlord? How do I find a rental property? How do I find a qualified tenant? What if the tenants tear up my house? What paperwork do I need?

The more informed you are going in, the more confident you will be, the more fun you will have, and the better your chance of enjoying and profiting greatly from the process.

There's truly never been a better time to be a landlord.

What's inside?

If you're new to landlording, you will learn a whole new language. Don't panic! With the easy discussion and instruction here, in no time you'll feel comfortable with how to own properties and manage tenants.

For ease of use, this book is divided into sections that allow you to read from beginning to end, or to jump around easily to specific topics. And for your convenience, definitions and an index of frequently used terms appears at the end of this book providing quick and easy reference.

Welcome to landlording!

Section One

GETTING STARTED

Owning real estate is, and historically has been, the No. 1 way to create long-term wealth in this country. You're at the perfect time in history because there's never been more opportunity for buying up properties at tremendous discount and filling them with tenants.

But to be successful, you need to understand some fundamentals, such as how to price your rental to keep it occupied and to receive maximum financial return, what steps are necessary to make it "tenant ready," how to market it, and how you determine a qualified prospective tenant.

So much to do even before you have a tenant! But this is the easy part, so let's get started.

Chapter 1

THIS IS A GREAT TIME TO BE A LANDLORD!

This is a *GREAT* time to be a landlord. And the facts prove my belief.

Since the housing meltdown, nearly 3 million new households have become renters. At least 3 million more are expected to join the ranks of renters by 2015. Many families no longer qualify for home loans and many who've owned homes in the past now find themselves renting as tenants.

The combination of low vacancies, increasing rental rates, and affordable properties makes this the perfect time to buy and own rental real estate.

The combination of low vacancies, increasing rental rates, and affordable properties makes this the perfect time to buy and own rental real estate. In today's market, you have the potential for strong and long-term cash flow combined with the promise of future appreciation.

In our lifetimes, there has never been a better time to buy real estate. Even in strong areas, you can easily offer 85 percent of retail value and purchase a property. When you add to that the incredibly low interest rates for financing, this is the perfect time to buy.

Values are low, but they won't stay there. There will be no more land in twenty-five years than there is right now. Odds are that, if you buy a house today, in as little as three to five years it will be worth more than it is right now. For landlords, rents will be higher in three to five years than they are today, but don't forget, your mortgage payment won't be.

So, if you're looking for a new way to produce income as well as a way to create future wealth and the ability to retire financially secure, invest in real estate.

Why others are investing

Don't just take my word for it. I asked some of our coaching students for reasons they are investing. Here are some of their answers:

> "Every year *Forbes* magazine produces a list of the top 100 wealthiest individuals in the USA. Somewhere around 20 percent of the top 100 invest in real estate.
>
> "Also, real estate remains one of the most 'protected' opportunities in that tax law, and political realities keep the real estate market among the most lucrative of all markets. This means that there is money to be made in both up and down markets." *Fred*
>
> "From my past experiences buying, fixing up, and selling the homes I've lived in came the realization that the source of the greatest return of any investment I've ever bought was through real estate. I never seriously considered making real estate investment a full-time career until the recent bottoming out of home prices coupled with the discovery of

Tax law and political realities keep the real estate market among the most lucrative of all markets. This means that there is money to be made in both up and down markets.

the Mastermind group. The opportunity of a lifetime presents itself along with the means to obtain it . . . what great fortune is that?" *Chuck*

"Real Estate is the only real thing that has stood the test of time for return on money that gives long term wealth. It is also a vehicle where you can be as big or small as you want to be and have that wealth and income at the same time. As investors, we can also be a great benefit to those looking to sell or buy homes. EVERYTHING in one package where everyone WINS." *Martin*

"Ability to build passive income along with big tax advantages." *Phil*

"All-in-all, real estate is one of the simplest ways to build wealth—or simply add supplemental income—without increasing hours away from home with a part-time job. Real estate continues to work, even on holidays and weekends. And, there are contingencies when problems arise, such as insurance when there is property damage. Even if that age-old adage about dealing with a stopped-up toilet in the middle of the night were to come true, that kind of problem happens only once in a while. *And,* you can choose to handle it yourself (one night of plumbing easily equals a week of a part-time job) or, even better, call a professional and savings from prior income should cover the cost." *Andy*

"For me, I've always had an interest in real estate. As I started to read books, attend seminars, and listen to webinars to educate myself, it became evident that real estate investing was one of the greatest ways to create wealth, and it was less risky than most other types of investments because you have a tangible asset as collateral. I initially thought I would just buy a few rental properties to supplement our income and create passive income for retirement, but the more strategies I learned the more excited I became about the potential for a full-time career. I believe if you are flexible and change with the times, you can make money in any kind of economy. Plus, it is the one last areas that have significant tax benefits.

"Last, I love the idea of being able to control my own destiny. When you've worked hard for other people all your life, having the autonomy to work when and how much you want is very liberating." *Carolyn*

I love the idea of being able to control my own destiny.

Owning rental properties—pros and cons

RENTING—PROS

- Renting out your property prevents selling now at a loss or losing it to foreclosure.
- Renting your home should cover your costs of ownership so you can move on without the concern of that overhead.
- Renting, over time, creates an income stream for you and your family.
- Someone else is paying down your mortgage.
- Owning rental property gives you added tax deductions.
- The property will provide income for your retirement.

- We're in a buyer's market, with more homes for sale than there are buyers to buy meaning (1) if you can't sell your property, rent it out and (2) you can buy rental properties at tremendous discounts.
- Fewer people are able to qualify for home loans because borrowing requirements have tightened, meaning, even if someone wants to buy, he or she may not be able to.
- The number of people preferring to rent homes instead of owning is increasing.

RENTING—CONS

- Dealing with tenants. (Yup, that's the big one.)
- Tenants could damage your property. (We hear this concern a lot but, fortunately, it never deterred us. Ninety-five percent of all tenant "damage" is normal wear and tear and the costs to maintain a rental property are, over time, much lower than the value gained.)
- If you continue to try to sell your home while tenant occupied, it could create challenges.
- If your rental house is also for sale, it may be more difficult to rent out if potential tenants know that potential buyers will be walking through and the house could be sold out from under them at any moment.
- Potential legal issues from dealing with tenants.

Chapter 2

SECURING YOUR RETIREMENT

We teach a presentation entitled "How to Secure Your Financial Retirement in as Little as Three Years." It goes something like this chapter.

The government is broke

What does this mean for you and, more importantly, for your retirement?

Are you counting on Social Security benefits for retirement income? Your 401(k)? Medicare and Medicaid? Should you be? Probably not the best plan.

So, what should you do instead?

Rental properties

Here's the process. If you buy three $100,000 properties per year for three years (nine $100,000 houses), you will conservatively have $1.96 million dollars net worth, and $18,000 per month income in twenty years or less. Add a total net cash flow from those nine properties over twenty years of approximately $1,050,000.

All of this can be done in your spare time while you maintain your forty-hour-per-week job. Of course, you can do more or less; you decide what's right for you.

Cash flow

Purchase properties that provide a minimum $200 per month cash flow after all property expenses. What does this mean? If your cost to own the home is $800 per month (this includes mortgage + interest on the loan + property taxes + property insurance, all totaled together), you must be able to collect a minimum of $1,000 per month rent. This "extra" $200 per month will cover added costs to you, such as replacing the water heater, or carpet and paint when tenants move out.

Purchase properties that provide a minimum $200 per month cash flow after all property expenses.

Before purchasing any rental property, you must know what your costs to own it will be, and you must determine how much rent you can charge once you own it with the goal of reaching that $200 per month. If costs to own the property (mortgage, interest, taxes, and insurance) are too high for the rent to cover your expenses plus the $200 additional each month, look for another house. Determining your costs to own and how much rent you can charge will be covered in more detail in Chapter 4.

This $200 "extra" will grow over time as you increase rents, but your mortgage payments will remain the same. This means, year after year, you will make more monthly profit on each property. This is assuming you receive a fixed interest rate on your mortgage. If you get an adjustable interest rate, be sure you know what you're doing and what your maximum costs for the loan will be.

Acquiring properties

The topic of buying properties is too complex to go into in great detail here. If you have questions, I recommend one of my other books, *The Essential Handbook for Buying a Home*. In the meantime, I will spend my time in this book teaching you how to manage the ones you have.

There are many different strategies for buying, including cash, seller financing, and acquiring the funds through partnerships. Some of the properties you'll acquire will need renovating while others will need only a new set of keys. Our criteria are that it must be purchased with equity and be guaranteed to provide cash flow from the day the tenant moves in. In today's real estate market, there are more properties that meet these criteria than you can purchase in one lifetime, so start buying!

What and where to buy

Purchase properties in stable neighborhoods and preferably with good school districts.

I believe strongly that the best way to grow your business is to keep it local. Everything we own is within a nine-mile radius of where we currently live. The grass is not greener far away. Buy local, where you know the market inside and out, and you will better be able to control your properties and your tenants.

Three-bedroom, two-bath homes are considered "bread and butter homes," as this is where most of America lives. Two bedrooms are harder to rent than three bedrooms because the largest percentage of residents have children and need the extra space. Even single people and married couples want the extra space of a third bedroom for an office or for guests. Yards are also preferred by most over apartment living.

Three-bedroom, two-bath homes are considered "bread and butter homes," as this is where most of America lives.

And, everyone wants at least two full bathrooms. Full bathrooms include toilet, sink, and tub. Half baths include toilet and sink but no tub. The No. 1 choice is two full baths and one half bath for guests, but the half bath is an extra and not necessary in your purchase.

Benefits to owning rental property

1. Someone else, your tenant, is making your mortgage payments for you.
2. You get all the tax advantages.
3. You receive monthly cash flow and your cash flow increases year over year as rents go up. While rents go up, your mortgage balance is going down. Eventually, you will owe nothing on the mortgage and 100 percent of the monthly rent payments will be income for you.

"But what if the tenant tears up the house?"

A question I hear ALL the time. My answer: Most tenants won't. Just like the people you know in your everyday life, most are responsible. We expect about 5 percent of the tenants to cause problems. As a general rule, when someone moves out of a property, the repairs needed are cosmetic only, typically carpet and paint.

> *Don't let concerns about damage keep you from investing in an asset that can make you tens or hundreds of thousands of dollars over time.*

And most costs are far, far less than the value you receive owning the property. If, for example, someone breaks a door and you have to replace it, most doors can be replaced for less than $75. If someone knocks a hole in the wall, it can be repaired and painted for no more than $50. Don't let concerns about damage keep you from investing in an asset that can make you tens or hundreds of thousands of dollars over time.

Tax benefits

To learn your true tax advantage, seek out an experienced real estate CPA or tax advisor. Depending upon your involvement in the business, you will be classified with either professional real estate status or passive real estate status. Basically, to qualify for professional real estate status, you must work in the business 750 hours per year, and more than half of your working hours must be in real estate. The tax advantages can be many and far reaching, but many factors are considered to allow for the different status qualifications. Learn these requirements from a qualified real estate CPA and establish what works best for you.

The IRS allows for depreciation of investment properties owned by taxpayers who can claim professional real estate status. The allowance reduces your taxable income by up to $2,900 per $100,000 of established property value for as long as 27.5 years.

To give you some idea, following is a basic example:

You own nine houses valued at $100,000 each (not including land value). Assuming the maximum allowance of $2,900, your taxes are reduced by nine times $2,900, or $26,100 per year for up to 27.5 years. This gives a total possible $717,750 deducted against your taxable income over 27.5 years.

If you don't qualify for professional real estate status on your tax return, but you do qualify as a passive investor, you are limited to $25,000 per year, or $687,500 over 27.5 years.

No matter how you slice it, owning real estate can add up to a LOT of tax savings!

Show me the numbers

- Purchase three $100,000 properties per year for three years (a very manageable pace).

- Acquire the properties at 15 percent below market value (not difficult, especially in today's real estate economy).
- Assume these properties appreciate at 4 percent per year. (This is an average over time. It may be lower in the next few years, but when the market turns around, and historically it always has, there will be a larger than 4 percent increase for some time.)
- Rents are calculated at 1 percent of property value per month (i.e., $1,000 for a $100,000 home).
- Rents are increased 4 percent annually at renewal (a very conservative increase).

Year 20:
Value $1.96 million
Equity $1.11 million
Net cash flow $108,000 to $200,000+ per year
Total net cash flow for 20 years $1,050,000

Are you convinced? Let's jump into the nuts and bolts of securing your financial future by becoming a landlord.

Chapter 3

WHO ARE YOUR TENANTS?

Before purchasing your property, it's important to decide where you want to own rental properties and which type of tenant you prefer.

Will you be marketing to the elderly, college students, young couples, families? Some landlords prefer owning mobile homes; some want apartments or multi-units; we prefer single-family homes. For the best use of your time and resources, both your properties and your marketing need to be directed toward the resident you prefer.

Single moms

Among renters, single moms had the biggest growth among household types between 2000 and 2010, according to census data analyzed by Property and Portfolio Research. This makes them an important audience for you to consider.

In fact, 40 percent of all children are now born to single moms, meaning that single mother households make up a major portion of the market for both buying and renting homes. Single moms tend to rent rather than buy because of many factors, including the costs associated with buying a home and the fact that renting comes with far fewer maintenance responsibilities.

Age and income

Most renters are middle aged, between 35 and 64, comprising the largest share of all American households.

Married couples (with and without children) make up 26 percent of all renters, single moms and single women together comprise close to 40 percent.

You may also decide to target a specific income based on the price of the properties you purchase. All of these factors come into play when you are considering your property purchases and marketing.

Know your audience

We had a very interesting experience when we started buying rental properties. In my mind, tenants lived in properties valued at less than $100,000. Price point varies, of course, depending upon your location. In our area at that time, we could purchase a nice brick, three-bedroom, one- or two-bathroom house in a decent neighborhood for $65,000 to $80,000. Rents were around $700 to $800 per month. We started out buying rental properties in this price range because, again, this was my image of a typical renter plus we knew we could pay the mortgage—$500 to $600 per month—out of pocket if the properties were vacant.

When we began buying as a full-time enterprise, we put up a nice website to capture leads and to communicate with potential clients. We had online prospects fill in a questionnaire telling us where they wanted to live, how many bedrooms and baths they needed, how much they could afford to pay per month, and how much they had to put down.

To our amazement, the majority of responses told us that they could pay $1,200 to $1,400 per month and had $3,000 to $5,000 to put down. We were not buying expensive enough houses! In one month, because of this market feedback, we jumped from buying $100,000 houses to $200,000 houses and had no problem filling them.

In sales, it is critical to know your target audience and to craft your product to meet their needs. Armed with this information, how will it affect how you market and what you buy?

In sales, it is critical to know your target audience and to craft your product to meet their needs.

Chapter 4

FINDING A PROPERTY AND DETERMINING ITS RENTAL VALUE

Where and what should you own to be a successful landlord? Additionally, how much rent should you charge and how do you know?

What type of property should you buy?

- **Buy where people want to live.** To keep your properties filled, especially starting out, avoid remote locations. People want to live near where they work and play. Most people want to live in safe neighborhoods, near convenient shopping and good schools, with easy access to major highways. Buy where populations are higher.

- **Buy in areas you know.** Don't guess about an area or purchase in a location someone suggests—know your market. Pick two or three neighborhoods near your home or office.

Areas you know are easiest for keeping up with statistics such as crime, property values, and rental and vacancy rates.

Focus exclusively on three separate neighborhoods—focus, study, and buy there—and ignore the rest.

When starting out, I knew a little bit about the neighborhood I lived in, nothing about any others. Trying to search through for-sale marketing and determine locations was overwhelming. I decided, almost immediately, to focus exclusively on three separate neighborhoods—focus, study, and buy there—and ignore the rest.

- **Own properties near where you live.** This makes filling and maintaining properties much easier. You want something nearby because you'll be driving by, especially when the properties are vacant, to check on your investment, to put out signs when marketing, to meet potential tenants, and, if you plan to manage it yourself, to do repairs.

  One of my first purchases was a forty-five minute drive from my house. Running by daily to check renovations, put out marketing flyers, and make sure lights were off and doors were locked took away too much of my limited, valuable time. I decided never to do that again. After the third tenant left that property, I sold it. Because I live in such a populated area, all of the homes I purchase are within ten minutes of my home and office.

- **Buy homes that have three bedrooms and two baths or larger.** Two bedrooms are much harder to rent out than three. Most of your potential clients will have children, and even single people or couples without children want extra space. And, it's hard to find a tenant who is satisfied with only one bathroom. Even single residents prefer at least an additional half bath for guests.

My least expensive rental is $600 per month. It's a small two-bedroom, one bathroom house. I'm constantly amazed, when it's vacant, at the number of potential clients who refuse to look at it because it has only one bathroom. At that price, I would think most houses have only one bathroom. Guess not!

- **Make sure your property will provide cash flow of at least $200 per month.** Before you purchase, know all of your costs to own the property and be sure you can get at least $200 more than that for your rent. A profit of $200 per month won't make you rich today. That money is to cover your costs of owning, such as a new hot water heater, new roof, or new carpet and paint when a tenant moves out.

  I have never made a purchase that did not provide cash flow from the day I closed on it. I have known other investors, however, who purchase for equity even if they can't get enough rent to cover their monthly expenses. It may seem tempting, but let me warn you, they learn that you can't eat equity and taking money out of your pocket every single month to cover expenses can stop your business growth in a hurry.

Investors quickly learn that you can't eat equity and taking money out of your pocket every single month to cover expenses can stop your business growth in a hurry.

- **Don't buy unless it provides cash flow from the day you purchase.** *Never bet on the future.* Don't buy thinking that rents will eventually go up. They may, but that doesn't help you out today. Don't buy because you think the house will be worth more in the future. Perhaps, but that kind of speculation hurt a lot of people in recent years. There are plenty of great deals that will provide solid cash flow from the day you purchase. If you're looking at one that won't, move on.

- **Don't tie up a lot of cash in a property you're planning to hold onto.** This is especially true for beginners. As investors, we recommend that our students flip (resell quickly) any properties they have a lot of cash in from purchase or renovation, and use the cash from that one property to buy several additional properties they can hold. This is a wonderful time to acquire rentals at great prices. When looking at distressed properties (properties that need a lot of fix-up), buy those at enough of a discount to allow for necessary repairs, and then resell at a quick profit.

- **Recognize that wealth in real estate comes over time.** You won't get wealthy early on from the cash flow off your rentals. What will create long-term, lasting wealth is having all the mortgages paid down over time, getting the tax write-offs rental properties provide, and increasing cash flow as you owe less year after year while rents continue to increase.

What is your cost to own the home?

A number of things need to be considered when determining how much rent to charge. Not the least of your concerns should be your costs to own the home. If you haven't paid off the mortgage, then your goal will be for the tenant to cover all costs to own the house and, hopefully, some extra for maintenance and cash flow.

Let's start there. What does it cost you to own the property? Add together your mortgage payment, the monthly interest charged on your loan, your property taxes (monthly), and any insurance you have on the property (this may include mortgage insurance as well as property insurance).

Once you've added those numbers together, you have established the lowest amount you can charge monthly for rent—enough to cover your costs.

Ideally, you want to add at least $200 to that monthly amount when calculating rent. Why? The extra $200 is not income so don't run out and spend it when it comes in. That extra $200 per month is to be set aside for maintenance on the property while the tenant lives there as well as any repair costs you encounter between tenants.

Four main property factors that determine how much rent you can charge:

- Location
- Size
- Number (and location) of bedrooms and bathrooms
- Condition

Beyond these, of primary concern to you as the owner is how much you must receive every month to break even and, hopefully, make a profit. To determine that amount, you must know your PITI. How much do you pay every month to cover the following:

Of primary concern is how much you must receive every month to break even and make a profit.

- The **principle** payments to your mortgage holder
- The **interest** you pay on that amount
- Your property **taxes**
- Possibly mortgage **insurance**

What if you can't charge enough to cover your costs?

If the rental amount is at least close to your cost of owning, it should allow you to put in a tenant who will contribute to your expenses, help pay down your mortgage, and allow you to receive tax benefits while they rent. Annual rental increases will eventually get payments to a place where they cover your expenses and, finally, generate profit. Remember, rents will increase over time but your mortgage payments will not, so eventually your tenants will be paying more for the property than you do!

If you haven't yet made a purchase I highly suggest, especially starting out, that you purchase a property where the monthly rental amount will more than cover your expenses. It's never good to own a property that takes money out of your pocket every month. There are plenty of homes on the market, so buy a property that will provide cash flow.

Setting rental pricing is important

Investigate your competition before you decide on your rental amount. You may even consider getting a professional appraiser's value before setting your price.

Studies show that pricing too far outside the local market can actually leave your home vacant longer. Too high is never good and too low makes buyers think something is wrong with the property.

Houses get the most attention the first two to six weeks they are on the market. Prospects constantly search for new listings and, if you house doesn't rent, prospective tenants and neighbors question what's wrong with your property. Be sure to price accurately from the beginning.

Find out what other properties in the area rent for

There are many online sites that allow you to type in the address and find rents for similar homes in your surrounding area. Here are a few sites to try:

- RentRange.com
- Rent-o-Meter.com
- RentBits.com

Increase the rental value of your home

Now that you know what your property will rent for, there are things you can do to raise the value and, therefore, the rental amount.

- **Appliances**. You can charge more if the home comes with appliances. Appliances can be purchased fairly inexpensively and they all add value to a rental. Many tenants can't afford to purchase their own, but would be willing to pay more per month if your home includes them already.

Many tenants can't afford to purchase appliances but would be willing to pay more per month if your home includes them.

- **Bedrooms**. Three bedrooms rent for more than two bedrooms; typically, four bedrooms rent for more than three. Is it possible for you to make an area in the home into an additional bedroom? The old home office spaces, for example, are obsolete thanks to laptop computers. Better to pull out built-ins and market another bedroom rather than a home office.

- **Bathrooms**. Definitely increase rental value. Perhaps there is a spare closet or space where a bath or even a half bath can be added.

- **Carports and garages**. You may have a decision to make about converting a garage to an additional bedroom. Depending upon the size of the house and the type of neighborhood, that is not always the best decision. Adding a carport may be a good economical decision. However, if you add a garage, it may take a long time to make the investment back.

- **Fences**. Most residents prefer a fenced yard. If you decide to install a fence, be sure to check with any homeowners associations in your neighborhood to make sure you stay within their restrictions (location, height, color, etc.).

- **Landscaping**. Also increases value. When prospects pull up to your house, you want them to see it as a home, their home, so attractive plantings are worth the investment.

- **Maintenance**. Naturally, you will attract tenants faster and more easily when the property is clean and well maintained. Before marketing the house, make sure that all needed repairs are complete and everything is sparkling clean. If you're not going to paint and put in new carpet, at least have the carpets cleaned so prospects can tell it's been done by the markings from the shampooer.

You've done all you can to add value and set your rental price, now let's get it ready to show.

Chapter 5

PREPARING YOUR PROPERTY

Renting out a property is very much like selling it. You don't need to do quite as much to the property to get it rented as to get it sold, but to fill it as quickly as possible, it's best to have it move-in ready. Spending $300 to get your property clean and ready for market is a much better investment than leaving it as-is and making another mortgage payment. Serious customers typically don't look at properties until they're ready to move, so if it's not move-in ready, potential prospects may walk through and walk away!

Basic repairs and updates

If your property needs updates, the time to do them is before and between tenants. When the property is vacant, see what needs attention and take care of it. No matter how large or small the needed repairs are, it's always easier to do them on a vacant property.

This also shows your tenants, from the beginning, that they'll be working with a landlord who cares. When they see how you expect the property to look, they're more likely to maintain your standard and know what you're looking for if you complain about theirs.

To get that property rented

- Make sure prospects can reach you, or someone working for you, anytime they call. The worst use of your marketing dollar is to get the phone to ring and then not be available to answer it.

Make sure prospects can reach you, or someone working for you, anytime they call.

- Have your properties 100 percent ready before showing them. Having a property that is repaired and clean is just as important as price in getting them rented.
- Have clean carpets—nothing torn—and new vinyl where needed. Always replace torn, stained, stretched, or faded vinyl.
- Bathrooms and kitchen should sparkle, including appliances.
- Replace all burned-out light bulbs.
- Become your prospective resident. Call and visit rental homes and apartments in your area to see what your competition looks like.
- Have friends or neighbors come by your property to give their feedback.

Know your competition

What prices and amenities are being offered? One free month's rent, free cable, water included? What can you do to compete?

Basic to-do's before you begin your marketing:

1. **Curb appeal**. No matter what the season, have the yard mowed, trimmed, and neat and have anything dead removed. It looks more inviting to prospects and, if the property looks like it will take a lot of work to keep up before they've even walked through the door, they're already discouraged.

2. **Front door**. At the very least, make sure it's clean. Make sure storm doors are clean and that all locks and door handles are functioning. A loose or broken lock gives a bad impression before prospects even enter your home. And, if you don't appear interested in taking care of it, they won't feel they need to, either.

3. **Light**. You want your home to look spacious and light. Make sure all bulbs in the house work. When the house is being shown, have ALL lights on, even closet lights and the one over the stove. Light and bright makes your home much more desirable.

4. **Windows**. Open blinds to let in as much natural light as possible. Take down all worn, or broken blinds. Bare windows look far better than windows with torn or broken treatments.

5. **Clean**. Have the home clean. If you don't plan to paint the entire interior and replace all the carpets, make sure what is there is clean.

6. **Smell/fragrance/odor**. This will be the first thing prospects notice when they walk in. You certainly don't want the house to smell musty (could indicate mold) or like the last tenant's pets. Consider lemon scented cleaning products or vanilla scented candles. If having trouble removing pet odors, the carpets may need to be replaced. Make sure all air filters have been changed. You may need to purchase an Ionizer and let it run until the odor is removed. After

one of our tenants vacated the property, there was so much damage and odor from pets that we even had professionals come out to clean the ductwork.

7. **Bathrooms**. Bathrooms should be clean. Make sure all light bulbs are working and the highest wattage possible. No one likes a dingy or dirty bathroom. Again, you want all prospects to know that you care for your property and the message you're giving them is that you will expect the same condition when they move out.

8. **Kitchen**. Clean all appliances. Let tenants know they should be in the same condition upon move-out.

Appliances

Because appliances tend to break down (usually from neglect, not age) and are so often stolen when tenants move out, decide whether or not you plan to supply them. Our homes come with a stove and oven and most come with built-in dishwashers, but supplying refrigerators is optional and we don't supply washers or dryers.

Here, your state law comes into play. Most states require provision of a stove and oven only. In some states, if it is in the property when the resident moves in, the landlord is responsible to maintain it. If you rent to Section 8 residents, it is absolutely the landlord's responsibility to maintain working condition on anything that is in the property when the tenant moves in.

You decide whether you want to provide appliances and increase your rent accordingly, or not provide them to eliminate responsibility. Some landlords provide appliances and charge additional fees for them. Know your state laws.

Section Two

FILLING PROPERTIES

No tenant = no income. Let's get that property filled.

Chapter 6

MARKETING

Got tenants? You can't fill your vacancy if prospects don't know what you have or that it's available.

If you don't understand marketing, you may have trouble reaching your audience. Look through newspapers, Craigslist, and other advertisements for the words, photos, colors, etc., that catch your eye, negatively or positively. What do you learn that you can incorporate into or omit from your marketing?

You can't fill your vacancy if prospects don't know what you have or that it's available.

Do prospects know your house is available?

Here are some ways to make sure they do:

- **Yard sign**. Where possible, have a sign in the yard that will be noticed by those who are driving by. Include a phone number *that someone answers*! Some homeowners associations don't allow yard signage, but be sure to place a sign in the window if you can't have one outside.

- **Flyer box**. Have the property information available in a flyer box in front of the house. Flyer boxes market anytime someone drives by.
- **MLS**. Have your property listed on the multiple listing service with fabulous photos and an outstanding description of the most desirable features. Yes, even rental properties can be put in the MLS. If you're not working with an agent, there are agents or companies who charge a flat fee to put properties on the MLS. This exposure helps your house be found through online searches.
- **Newspaper ads**. Fewer people are reading newspapers so this may not be the best choice for your marketing dollars. Are you targeting an older demographic? If so, you may still need to consider newspaper advertising.
- **Online listing sites.** There are tons of free online listing sites (free is good). Zillow.com and Trulia.com are just two to get you started.
- **Neighbors**. Put out flyers and talk to neighbors and co-workers about your house. Neighbors are a huge source of referrals. We've even had neighbors prefer our house over the one they were renting down the street, so they gave their notice and moved into ours. You never know who's looking!
- **Local companies**. If you own properties near a large company, ask their human resource department about any need for corporate housing. Often, companies seek temporary housing for employees who are not in town full time and need furnished housing.
- **Finder's gifts.** Offer a finder's gift if someone refers the person who buys your home (i.e., $250, a gift card, a microwave).

- **Don't blend in**. What can you do above and beyond the usual that makes your property get attention? Why would someone find you in the stack of homes for rent?

Being proactive is absolutely necessary to find a qualified tenant. The good news is that it's easier than ever today with all the available online help.

Tips for effective marketing

- **Describe both features and benefits.** Always include both in your ad. Most landlords list "features," such as the number of bedrooms and bathrooms, but leave out "benefits." Benefits include being close to shopping and dining or major highways, desirable school district, nearby parks and lakes, etc.
- **Good photos.** Always include the maximum number allowed. Prospects do a lot of shopping online, so make sure you have plenty of crisp, clear photos in your ads.
- **Craigslist.** This service is free and available all over the country. Read other ads for ideas; see which ones stand out to you and why. Be sure to add the maximum number of photos. You'll need to update your ad on Craigslist every two to three days as they quickly fall down the list of newly placed rentals, but this is one of the most frequented sites and it's FREE!
- **Newspapers.** We find newspapers to be expensive and fairly ineffective. It's hard to make your property stand out from the crowd in a newspaper. And a huge portion of the population no longer reads

Make sure all of your marketing has your contact information.

newspapers. There are many more effective and less expensive ways to market your home.

- **Contact information**. Another tip that seems obvious: Make sure all of your marketing has your contact information. I've picked up more than one marketing flyer from an information box only to later realize that it had the property address but no way to contact an owner.

Be sure ALL marketing includes

- The property address
- Photos
- Description details (number of bedrooms and baths, square footage, etc.)
- Benefits (schools, shopping, etc.)
- A contact name, phone number, and e-mail address

Additional marketing ideas

First and foremost in getting a property rented—anywhere, in any condition—is marketing. Putting a sign in the yard and hoping a passerby takes your home is one strategy. Here are some additional ideas to add to get that house filled!

- **Lighted signage**. Illuminate your signs even after dark to catch people driving home late.
- **Take-aways**. At open house (yes I do open houses for rentals) hand out something

Coupons for local merchants are great give-aways and help prospects learn what's available nearby.

your lookers will remember, something that will be a positive reminder of your home. Hand out bottles of water, flyers about your property, and any local information you can provide. Coupons for local merchants are great giveaways and help prospects learn what's available nearby.

- **Information flyer**. Create a flyer with all the local conveniences you can find: shopping, schools, universities, hospitals, malls, restaurants, gas stations, attractions in the area, local police and fire stations, even school bus pick-up locations. Assume your lookers don't know the neighborhood.
- **Voicemail.** Be available! Consider adding a phone number to your family plan that you can use in your marketing. Or, if you plan to use your existing phone number, be sure to add a voice mail message with property information and assurance that you will get back to the caller as soon as possible.
- **Neighborhood letters**. Send letters to the neighbors inviting them to "pick their neighbor" with information about your home and the open house. Give them an incentive to talk about it to others (i.e., $200 gift card if they find your buyer). We mail between two hundred fifty and four hundred fifty letters to surrounding homes telling neighbors the day and time of our open house.
- **Signs**. Put signs in the yard and add as many directional signs to your house as the neighborhood allows. Make it easy for passersby to find your house.
- **Flyers**. Put flyers out in surrounding shopping areas, coffee shops, grocery stores, restaurants, motels, gyms, daycares, etc.
- **Market your house advantages**. Great schools, low crime, convenient to parks and major highways, great shopping, spectacular views, easy access to anything you can think of!

- **Description**. The words you use to describe your property are *very* important. Words like, "Move-in Ready," "Gorgeous," "Beautiful," and "Landscaping" really help!
- **Human resource departments**. E-mail HR departments at local companies. Many employees prefer to live close to their jobs but don't make time for house hunting. Make it easy for them to find yours!
- **Make your house sing!** Whatever you have, paint it, clean it, fix it, make sure it works properly and looks great. That includes the yard, the exterior, and the interior.
- **Church bulletins**. Place notices in local church bulletins.
- **Neighborhood newsletters.** Many will let you place ads for free. Also check to see if they have a website where you can advertise.

Many neighborhood newsletters will let you place ads for free.

- **Apartment complexes.** Mail flyers advertising your advantages, such as a fenced yard.
- **Word of mouth**. Make sure all of your current residents know that you have properties available all of the time and that they can receive a gift for any referral who moves into one of your houses.
- **Colleges**. Contact university student housing departments if nearby.
- **Specials**. Offer holiday or monthly move-in specials and incentives. For example, December Special: "$100 off first month's rent if you move in before December 25th!"
- **Tenant newsletter**. A great way to keep in contact with your tenants and to share new information is to mail or email a

monthly newsletter. Include property information in your newsletters with photos of what's currently available.

- **Local merchants**. Ask if you can put up flyers in their store windows or on counters and offer to place their coupons or business info in your new resident flyers or to mention them in your monthly tenant newsletters.
- **Gift certificates**. Tell merchants that you will buy $25 or $50 gift certificates to their business if they refer a move-in client to you and use the certificate as a move-in special or incentive for residents.
- **Real estate agencies**. Let them know you have rentals available for their clients who might not be able to qualify now for financing.
- **Social media**. Market through social media: Facebook, Twitter, LinkedIn.
- **Give-aways**. Advertise that you are offering special give-aways to new residents or for dropping by your open houses.
- **Hospitals**. If you're close, be sure to advertise there, as doctors, nurses, and even janitorial staff want to live close to where they work.
- **Police**. Want a police car in your driveway? Advertise at the local police department and even offer discounts or incentives for police or fire officials.
- **For-rent signs**. Put them up even in your properties that have tenants. The signs generate calls and you can lead the caller to other properties you have available.
- **On the Web.** Use the many free marketing sites, such as Craigslist.com, Trulia.com, and Zillow.com.
- **Moving companies**. Let them know you rent properties. They often have clients coming to town.

- **Attitude!** Always assume everyone you speak with about your property is going to rent it. Your intention and attitude go a long way toward getting it sold.

- **Features**. Don't just show the available property, sell it! Be enthusiastic. Know the features and benefits. Be proud when you show it so the new resident will be proud when they move in!

Always assume everyone you speak with about your property is going to rent it. Your intention and attitude go a long way toward getting it filled.

- **Image**. Always be neat and well groomed. You need to present the same image you want your properties to convey and that you hope your new resident will project while living in your property.

- **Shopping centers**. Print flyers and distribute in shopping centers, Walmart, Home Depot, malls. Put on car windshields or pay someone to do it for you.

- **Group meetings**. If meeting a prospect at the property to show it, try to schedule more than one at the same time. It creates a feeling of scarcity and urgency.

- **Lockbox**. We put a lockbox on the door of all vacant properties and let prospects go through on their own. This eliminates unnecessary time on our part, especially for those prospects who make an appointment but don't show.

- **Testimonials**. Include quotations of what your current residents have to say about working with you on the back of property information sheets.

- **Welcome mat**. Place one at the entrance of your properties.

- **Virtual tour**. Walk through the vacant property and video as you point out the features and benefits. Upload the video to YouTube, your website, and other online marketing sites that let you use video.
- **Highlight features**. Ask prospects what they especially want in a rental and if yours has them, highlight those features as you show it!
- **Community information**. Provide prospects utility companies, cable companies, nearby shopping, and schools.
- **Applications**. Always carry applications with you when meeting a prospect or have them in a kitchen drawer if you allow prospects to view on their own.
- **Focus on the Positive.** Don't apologize for what you consider to be shortcomings with your property. Things you don't like may be just what they're looking for. For example, you may think the small kitchen is a negative, but the prospect may love the fact that everything will be within easy reach and it will be easy to keep clean. Always point out the positives!
- **Raise the price**. If you've done everything and it's clean, ready, and has great amenities but is not renting, raise the price! A higher price will bring out a whole new level of lookers who may see the value you're offering. If you get nothing after a couple of weeks, you can always drop the price again. Be sure your pricing is in line with others in the area.
- **Find out why.** If a prospect turns down your property, do all you can to find out the real reason. It may be something you can take care of before the next showing.
- **Ask for the money.** After a showing, ask when they plan to move in and if they prefer to pay the deposit by money order, bank check, or credit card. Always assume they plan to take it.

- **Offer an incentive.** If they sign the contracts within 24 hours of viewing the property, offer a financial incentive. It can be a discount off the move-in amount, a discount off a future month's rent, a gift card to a home improvement store, anything you come up with.

- **How did they find you?** Ask every prospect. Keep track of what marketing is working so you can focus there—and what isn't so you can improve or eliminate it. If you don't measure it, you can't improve it.

- **If it's already rented**. If someone responds to a property that is already taken, don't just hang up. Get this person's contact information, find out what he or she is looking for, and tell this prospective tenant about other properties you have or will have available.

- **Keep Marketing!** Even when all of your properties are filled, never stop marketing. Stay in contact with anyone who looked at a property but didn't take it. It's important to have a list of prospects anytime a property becomes available as this can dramatically cut down vacancy times. You will have more properties come available and you will need more tenants.

- **Finally, make sure your house is available to show at anytime.** Consider a lock box on the door so you can give out the code when someone is there and ready to view it. This puts you ahead of landlords who only show when it's convenient for them. If it's difficult to schedule an appointment, prospects will move onto the next home and the chances with them are lost. Be accommodating. Make your house readily available.

Make sure your house is available to show at anytime a prospect is ready to view it.

Number one way to keep your properties filled

The number one way to keep your properties filled is to keep your current residents happy. Don't lose the tenants you already have. Communicate, be available, care. Be the landlord you would want to have so your customers not only stay longer, but also refer you to all of their friends and family. Your satisfied current customers are the best marketing tool you'll ever have.

Chapter 7

OPEN HOUSE

If you want to rent out your property, prospects need to see the inside. Not a lot of landlords do open houses but I always have. They're free, so why not? Having an open house is a great way to get a number of prospects through on the same day, which creates energy and buzz.

I have open house on Sundays from 2 p.m. to 4 p.m. In our area, that's when most real estate agents have their open houses so that's when the public is out looking for them. Might as well make use of your local agent's marketing!

Why have an open house?

- To show off the property
- To show your home to multiple people who are interested in the house and the neighborhood at the same time
- To show it to the neighbors, who are always curious, and who may know someone wanting to live there
- To let people know your company has rental properties and to find out what they're looking for

- To create a prospect list for the next property you have coming available
- To let sellers know you may be interested in buying their rental property

Open house is never simply about the house you're showing.

Prospects have followed us online and come to multiple open houses until they found the one they liked. They follow us because they like the kinds of properties we own and the condition we have them in for move-in. I have signed up numerous tenants at open houses.

In fact, I've had more than one open house where prospects were actually competing for the property. They both came ready with cash. My rule, first one with completed and approved applications and all the funds needed to move in wins!

And I have, more than once, had neighbors come by and ask if I'd be interested in buying properties from them.

All marketing is good, but being able to get out and talk with the public is my favorite and, by far, some of my most productive. An open house is never simply about the house you're showing. It's a fabulous, and may I stress again FREE, marketing tool.

In case I have you convinced, here's how:

Getting prepared

For any house showing, have your home's best face ready.

1. **Clean up the yard.** Get rid of all debris—anything dead or dying. Cut back overgrowth. Rake the yard well and throw out new seed. Freshen up flower beds with bark or straw and plant flowering plants when the weather allows.

2. **Exterior touch up.** Make sure the front door looks fresh and the hardware is in good, functioning order. No loose or difficult door knobs.

3. **Interior touch up.** Clean carpets as needed. Clean moldings and switch plate covers. Sticky fixtures are not attractive to prospects. Remove or replace damaged blinds.

4. **Make sure the kitchen and bathrooms sparkle**. Just like you would want in a property you'd move into.

It's always worth the effort. If your home is ready to move into, your prospects will be more eager and more motivated to decide immediately in order to beat out any competition! And remember, you're showing them how you want the home maintained. If you care, it's more likely your tenant will care.

How to have an open house

Don't just put a sign in the yard and leave the door open. To be successful, there must be some preparation.

1. **Advertise.** Post notices of open house on the MLS, Postlets, Zillow, Trulia, (all of which feed to multiple websites), Craigslist, etc. Anywhere your house is listed, change the ad to include your open house, the date and times. If possible, advertise in neighborhood newsletters and websites.

2. **Mail a neighborhood letter**. The week of your open house, let the neighbors know that the house is now ready for occupancy and invite them to come by and take a look. They may prefer yours over one they're already renting!

   Again, open house is never just about the house you have available. This letter is a non-threatening way to let the neighborhood know who you are and what you do. Some of them may end up being your future tenants, sellers, or buyers.

The morning of the open house, tie balloons to the signs so they can't be missed.

3. **Directional open house signs**. Put up

signs, not only in the yard, but also throughout the neighborhood with directional arrows so passers by know there's an open house and how to find it. Be sure to have plenty of posted and well positioned signs from every neighborhood entry point. This is especially important if your home is near the back of the neighborhood.

A number of neighborhoods, especially the newer ones, have sign ordinances. Many areas only allow open house and directional signs from Friday afternoon to Monday morning. If that's the case, that's when you should put out all the directional arrow signs and the open house sign in the front yard. The morning of the open house, tie balloons to the signs so they can't be missed. Don't forget to pick up the signs when open house is over.

4. **Have the home and yard neat and tidy.** Even if you're leaving some of the fix up for the next tenants, the house and yard should be tidied up. You want prospects to see that you care so they will, too.

5. **Turn on all the lights.** Make sure all the bulbs work so the house looks bright and cheery. Open all blinds to let in natural light and expand the rooms with exterior views. Turn on ALL lights in the house including closets, under cabinets, and on the stove vent.

6. **Have a sign-in sheet.** Ask for visitor's name, e-mail address and phone number. Always follow up the next day to thank them for coming by, to see what they thought of the house, and to

Always follow up the next day to thank prospects for coming by, to see what they thought of the house, and to find out if they have additional questions.

find out if they have additional questions. Follow-up is very important to know what prospective tenants are looking for. This feedback really helped us change our buying strategies!

7. **Have a handout sheet** that includes a photo of the home (so they remember which house it is) and as many of the positive features as you can list. Many prospects will look at more than one house in the same day and can forget yours in a very short time without a photo and information sheet. Get flyers out of information tubes from homes that are for sale to use as your examples—then improve upon them!

8. **Smell/odor/aroma.** Air out your home so it doesn't smell stuffy (could mean mold) or like pets.

9. **What time to hold your open house.** I hold open house on Sunday from 2 p.m. to 4 p.m. because that's standard in our area for real estate agent open houses. Most of the public is trained to be out at those hours looking for open houses so I want to capture that already existing viewer. I have done the same hours on Saturday when the property is located in a high traffic area and I can be assured of good turnout even without advertising ahead of time. My Saturday marketing is simply directional signs and balloons.

10. **One last tip.** Make sure you have toilet paper in the house. I believe that, in every open house I've had, someone used the restroom!

Your enthusiasm for the home helps to rent it.

Keep your open house simple so you're fresh and excited about it. Your enthusiasm for the home helps to rent it. Not everyone will have positive things to say, but remember, it only takes one person who loves it to get it filled.

Good luck. Open houses work.

Chapter 8

THE APPLICATION

Always take an application from your potential residents. This provides you with all of their contact and personal information and gives you the ability to check them out before you move them in.

When do they fill out an application?

Have your prospects fill out a rental application after they have looked at, and are interested in, the property. I always have applications at open house and I keep some at available properties in the kitchen drawer beside the sink or stove. That way if someone accesses the house on their own with the lock box, when they call back to say they're interested, they can immediately pick up an application right there at the house, fill it out, and fax or bring it in.

Always have applications at open house and keep some at available properties in the kitchen drawer beside the sink or stove.

You can use online applications, fax, or have the prospect come to your office or meeting location.

Application fee

Charge one. Find out what is allowed in your state. These fees are typically small, $25 to $50 per applicant, and can be refundable or nonrefundable. You may want to credit the fee amount to move in charges when your new tenant moves in, but keep the fee if the prospect is turned down because of screening results.

This is your first opportunity to screen your applicant's financial strength. Warning: If they balk or say they don't have the money for the application fee, they will later tell you they don't have the money for rent.

If they say they don't want to lose the money if they're turned down when you do their background check, they know something you don't about their background so you've saved yourself time and effort. If they ask you to waive the fee, this is a bad sign and you're establishing a pattern that may only get worse.

Every applicant 18 years or older who will be living in the property for any length of time must fill out an application.

And, yes, you deserve the fee. It will cover your time for doing the showing, interviewing, and ultimately the screening process. You will be charged a fee when you do credit and background checks online so this fee goes to recover those costs.

Who fills out an application?

Every potential resident, 18 years or older, who will be living in the property for any length of time must fill out an application. If someone new moves in at a later date, this person must fill out an application and be approved just like every other tenant. You must know who is living in your property or you will have no control when problems arise.

What's on the application

Things to ask for on the application:

- Name
- Current address
- Phone numbers
- E-mail address
- Social security number
- Date of birth
- Driver's license number
- Current landlord's name
- Current employer and contact information
- Length of time at job
- Income
- Credit references
- Personal references
- Emergency contacts
- Pet(s), including name(s), description(s), and weight(s)
- Automobile information: make, model, year, color, license plate number, monthly payment
- Signature and date

Along with the completed application, we ask for a copy of each applicant's driver's license or picture identification card, social security card, and latest pay check stub(s).

Must be filled out *completely*

Each prospect over 18 must fill out his or her own application *completely* and turn in all additional documents you require. Many applications state that any form not filled out *completely* will automatically be denied.

You need the information on this sheet for a reason so, no, they may not leave lines of their choice blank!

Filling out the completed application and presenting it with the required application fee is the first step in your screening process.

Chapter 9

TENANT SCREENING PROCESS

The screening process is necessary, the most important process a landlord does and can end up saving you time, money, and frustration.

You must investigate the tenant's background, rental and eviction history, credit reports, criminal reports, and proof of income to protect yourself before they move in. You are, after all, turning over to them a very expensive piece of real estate. You have a right to know who this person is before you hand over your keys.

You have a right to know who this person is before you hand over your keys.

We all want the tenant who pays on time, handles his or her own repairs, maintains a beautiful lawn, and is adored by the neighbors. But many tenants don't pay rent, call you for every flaw in the house (it's your house, after all), and refuse to mow "your" grass.

Believe me, I know how difficult it is to turn away an applicant who has cash in hand (the first few times), but the best thing you can do for your business could be to reject an under-qualified applicant.

Following the law

Following the law is not that difficult:

- Make sure your contracts are state and federal compliant.
- Have a detailed application with all your requirements spelled out.
- Have your own set of criteria for accepting tenants and apply these same set of criteria for every applicant. You can determine these for yourself, within the law. For example, you may choose to only accept applicants whose credit scores are over 600, have no criminal record, have never been evicted, have monthly gross income equal to three times the amount of rent, etc. However, consumer protection laws state that what you apply to one you must apply to all.

A landlord is legally free to set any conditions for tenancy as long as they don't violate anti-discrimination laws. The Federal Fair Housing Acts (42 U.S. Code § 3601–§ 3619) prohibit discrimination on the basis of race, color, religion, national origin, gender, age, familial status (having children), and physical or mental disability (including alcoholism and past drug addiction). Many states and cities also prohibit discrimination based on marital status or sexual orientation.

Running a credit check

We do and so should you. We don't expect our residents to have great credit; some in fact, have terrible credit. But, you can learn a lot more about your prospects by looking at their credit history than simply their credit score.

For example, does the social security number and address match what your prospect told you? If not, what else is he or she hiding? Does this person have a history of unpaid bills? If so, what makes you think he or she will pay you on time? Does your prospect have judgments for unpaid utility bills? When this tenant moves into your property, do you have any idea whose name the utilities will be in?

It's perfectly acceptable for you to pass along the cost you incur to run the credit and background checks. This is the reason we charge an application fee. Most states limit the amount per tenant. In every state, it is illegal for the landlord to take the fee and not run the check.

Charge the fee and run a credit check. You won't regret the investment.

For credit check resources, go to the Tenant Screening Sites listed under Internet Resource Links at the back of this book.

Doing a criminal background check

There are many online sites and services for performing this check. National Tenant Network is one to try. Shop around to compare fees and which services they provide. As in the case of your credit check, you won't regret making sure that your tenants have no outstanding legal issues.

Contacting present and past landlords

If the applicants don't want you to contact their current or past landlords, this is a warning. When they're moving, you hope their landlord knows. If they're sneaking away, they will do the same to you. And, don't let the applicant blame a landlord for their eviction or for not fixing things. If this is their conversation, it will be repeated when they leave you.

When you call to check past tenant behavior, be as certain as you can that you're talking with a landlord and not the applicant's friend or family member who happens to answer that phone number.

Get permission to contact employers

Contacting employers should not be a problem if there is no problem with the applicant. Employers may not wish to answer anonymous questions over the phone, so be prepared to e-mail or fax a list of questions from your website or on your letterhead.

In fact, have applicants give authorization to contact references, including emergency contacts, for rental consideration and for collection purposes should this be deemed necessary.

Have applicants give authorization to contact references, including emergency contacts, for rental consideration and for collection purposes should this be deemed necessary.

Proof of income

At the very beginning, make sure prospective tenants earn enough to afford your property. At least two and a half times what their rent will be per month is preferred. And, no, do not accept child support payments as income. I count child support as bonus money for tenants to cover unexpected things that will come up in their lives. Child support payments are inconsistent at best, and I don't want my tenant's excuse for not paying rent to be that an ex-husband or ex-wife didn't mail the payment this month.

Verify income. Get copies of the two most recent pay stubs and confirm the dates. If they don't get pay stubs, have them bring in copies of bank statements or even tax returns. If they don't have any of that, they have no income and how do you expect them to pay rent?

Tenant screening warnings

When you first meet a prospect and this person wants your property, he or she is typically on their best behavior. If you find any sign of potential problems now or even get a "gut" feeling, pay attention. It really may be better to reject an applicant than to accept him or her. Passing on an applicant up front may save you huge problems in the future.

When you first meet a prospect and this person wants your property, he or she is typically on their best behavior.

Here are some warning signals that should put you on alert:

1. They don't bring in the completed applications for either (a) themselves or (b) others who will be living in the home.
2. They don't want to pay the application fee. If this is a problem, believe me, rent will be a problem.
3. They don't bring the entire down payment, especially frustrating when they have assured you over the phone that they will.
4. They don't have the income needed to pay rent. Always verify income. No, the promise that a friend, family member, fiancé, etc., is going to help does not count. The applicants must qualify on their own unless they're students and a parent is qualifying (and paying) for the unit for them.
5. They want to give you less than you're asking for to hold the property.
6. They don't want you to run a criminal or background check. This is probably a good place to stop since you both understand that it's ultimately not going to be a good fit.
7. They're unemployed. No, unemployment checks do not qualify as income, even if it is enough to pay rent.
8. They talk negatively about their current landlord.

9. They don't have a car (unreliable transportation = unreliable income = unreliable rent—unless, perhaps, you live in New York City).

10. You call back and their phone number's been disconnected.

11. They complain because the house has both electric and gas and they don't want to pay two bills.

12. They "failed" the criminal background check.

13. They have the deposit, but they want you to hold it until they can come up with the first month's rent.

14. They ask if you'll accept less because, after all, they have to get their utilities turned on.

15. They don't have all the money because they want your place so much that they already put a deposit down on rental furniture and/or electronics.

16. They don't have all of the money for ANY reason.

I consider lack of funds the biggest issue. If they don't have the money starting out, what makes you think they'll have the money they owe you going forward? In my experience, the ones who have financial excuses going in are the ones I'm evicting for non-payment within the first six months (often, the second or third month).

If you have the opportunity to take the rental application in your potential tenants' current home, seeing how they live is a great way to see how they will eventually care for your property.

Yes, it's normal that people have problems, but don't let their problems become yours.

And, if you have the time or opportunity to take the rental application in your potential tenants' current home, seeing how they live is a great way to see how they will eventually care for your property. Looking inside their vehicle is also very telling.

Declining an applicant

Declining an applicant is perfectly acceptable. Some applicants actually expect it because they know more about their record and background than you do. And many landlords, with a structured screening process, reject more tenants than they accept.

If you reject an applicant because of information on a credit report, you are required to tell this person which agency the information came from. This is required by the federal Fair Credit Reporting Act (15 U.S. Code § 1681). You must also tell the person that they have a right to obtain a copy of the file from the agency that reported the negative information by requesting it within sixty days of being told that their rejection was based on a credit report. There could be an error on their report and they deserve the opportunity to correct it.

The main thing about declining someone is that you be consistent as to your reasons. The reason a tenant is declined is a business decision and should be because this person did not meet your criteria.

Chapter 10

LEASE WITH OPTION TO BUY

It's very possible you'll have an applicant come along who would, someday, love to own the house you have for rent. At this time, however, they're not able to qualify for a conventional bank loan. A lease with option to buy is the perfect way to sell while still maintaining ownership.

How is lease-to-own different from a rental?

Lease-to-own works very much like a rental, but with some of the benefits of buying. The buyer does not, however, need to qualify up front through a traditional lender.

With a lease-to-own, the lessee/tenant is actually working toward owning the home at a future date.

Similar to renting, the tenant/buyer (lessee) moves into your property and pays a monthly amount to live there. The difference with a lease-to-own is that the lessee/tenant is actually working toward owning that home at a future date, typically three years or less.

The contracts signed include terms for both the rental agreement and the lease agreement. The additional lease terms spell out conditions for the future purchase of the home such as:

1. The amount of time the lessee has to purchase (typically twelve to thirty-six months)
2. The purchase price of the home (which is locked in for the term of the contract)
3. The amount of the lease option fee (or "down payment" to move in)
4. Any possible seller financing terms
5. The amount of monthly credit toward purchase given for on-time payments; we typically credit 10 percent of all on-time premium monthly payments toward the purchase price
6. Any other terms or conditions of the lease

Contract features

With a lease-to-own, the "buyer" pays the monthly market rate rent plus an additional monthly rent premium. This negotiable rent premium, we charge 10 percent, is the amount that is credited every month toward the purchase price.

The lease option fee actually "buys" the lessee the right to purchase the home at a future date and locks in the purchase price.

The lease option fee actually "buys" the lessee the right to purchase the home at a future date and locks in the purchase price. It is required at time of contract signing, is generally one percent to five percent of the purchase price, and part or the entire lease option fee may be credited toward the purchase price at closing.

If the contract is not fulfilled, the lease option fee and any monthly rent premiums are forfeited and the "buyer" moves on or may stay in the property as a rental tenant only.

Benefits to buyer and seller

The great thing about a lease-to-own for the buyer/tenant/lessee is that they know they have a contract toward buying the home they live in. While the lease option is in effect, the home cannot be sold to someone else (which is one of the risks with a rental). This gives the lessee time to save a down payment and increase his or her credit score before applying for a loan. Also, the lease option fee plus the monthly rent premium are all building up the tenant's own equity in the home. And, if the tenant decides he or she doesn't like the house, the neighborhood, or even the neighbors, the buyer can move on at any time by not exercising this option.

When structured properly, a lease-to-own creates a win/win for both buyer and seller.

The great thing about a lease-to-own for the seller/lessor is that you have a tenant in place who is planning to purchase the property at a future date. Before the purchase is final, the seller maintains the advantages of cash flow, mortgage pay down, and tax benefits. Also, the tenant is paying the monthly rent premium and, if he or she moves without exercising the option to purchase, the option fee and premium payments are retained as income.

When structured properly, a lease-to-own creates a win/win for both buyer and seller.

Section Three

THE PAPERWORK

No job is done until the paperwork is complete. Make sure you not only have all the necessary forms and documents you'll need, but you must ensure that they are state and federal compliant. The majority of landlord/tenant laws are state specific, so, if you purchase contracts rather than having them created for you by a local real estate attorney, have them checked for compliance.

If you ever find yourself in court (and if you own rental properties, you will) the paperwork, when done correctly, can save you.

Chapter 11

DO YOU KNOW THE LAW?

Do you know the state and federal landlord/tenant laws? Are you aware of your state's building and housing codes? If you own rental properties, you'd better be informed. As is often said, if you're a landlord it's not a matter of "if" you go to court, it's a matter of "when."

Specifics vary by state, so know what your state allows and requires. Following are just a few of the more common rules:

TENANTS MUST:

- Pay rent, in full and on-time
- Take care of the property in a reasonable manner
- Not deliberately or negligently destroy, deface, damage, or remove any part of the premises or knowingly permit any person to do so
- Not sublet the property or take in additional residents without the landlord's written permission

LANDLORDS MUST:

- Comply with all current applicable building and housing codes, as well as with all state and federal landlord/tenant laws
- Not discriminate during the tenant selection process
- Put the lease agreement, including who pays for what utilities and who is responsible for what maintenance, in writing
- Keep the property in fit and habitable condition
- Keep all common areas of the premise in safe condition
- Provide operable smoke detectors in all units
- Allow the tenant privacy and "quiet enjoyment" of the property
- Notify tenants in writing if the property changes ownership
- Neither prevent the tenant's access to the property, nor turn off utilities
- Follow the legally specified notification process if requiring a tenant to vacate the property

Landlording forms and regulations

Two very helpful sites for landlord/tenant laws in all fifty states are the National Landlord Tenant Guides at RentLaw.com and Nolo.com.

I once used RentLaw to find out if tenants are allowed to simply call and tell me they'll "be out by the weekend." That's better, of course, than when they don't say they're leaving or when they simply don't pay and we have to go through the eviction process. But I did wonder. I'm pretty lenient with anyone who has been a good tenant and a good payer, but I want to know my rights as the landlord.

Abandonment of lease

So, when I looked it up at RentLaw.com, here's what I read:

"The lease is a contract between the landlord and the tenant. The tenant can get out of the lease only if the lease itself allows the tenant to do so and the tenant follows the procedures laid out in the lease. For example, the lease may permit the tenant to move out simply by giving notice thirty days in advance.

But there is no law that allows tenants to abandon any lease just by giving a notice thirty days in advance.

If the tenant abandons the premises prior to the expiration of the lease, the tenant will still have to pay rent every month until the landlord rents the premises to another tenant or the lease expires. This is called mitigating damages—the landlord is damaged when you break the lease until they re-rent the unit—for the same price, more, or less."

If the tenant abandons the premises prior to the expiration of the lease, the tenant will still have to pay rent every month until the landlord rents the premises to another tenant or the lease expires.

Clear and easy to understand. I love this site. It's packed with information.

Carbon monoxide detectors

Carbon monoxide is odorless, colorless, and tasteless. According to the Centers for Disease Control and Prevention, more than 400 people in the United States die from carbon monoxide poisoning each year.

Check your state laws to see if they require carbon monoxide detectors to be installed. Our state requires detectors in all rental units with fossil fuel appliances, fossil fuel fired heating systems, or an attached garage.

Homes built prior to 1978

If you remodel or repaint a home built prior 1978, you must get approval for your work by the Environmental Protection Agency (EPA) or face fines of up to $37,500 *per day*.

Federal law requires you or your contractor be certified and use lead-safe work practices. To become certified, renovation contractors must submit an application and fee payment to the EPA. Contractors performing renovation, repair, and painting projects that disturb lead-based paint in homes, child care facilities, or schools built before 1978 must be certified and must follow specific work practices to prevent lead contamination.

If you remodel or repaint a home built prior 1978, you must get approval for your work by the Environmental Protection Agency.

NOTE: Contractors and training providers working in Wisconsin, Iowa, North Carolina or Mississippi must contact the state to find out more about its training and certification requirements. These states are authorized to administer their own RRP (Renovate, Repair, Paint) programs in lieu of the federal program.

According to the EPA, "Anyone receiving compensation for renovating, repairing, and painting work in residences built before 1978 that disturbs painted surfaces is subject to the Renovation, Repair and Painting Rule."

Why? Mainly, to protect children from the effects of lead-based paint.

What's regulated? Almost every renovation including paint scraping, window replacement, and carpet removal (which can disrupt painted trim). Only minor interior repairs, less than 6 feet square in size, and exterior repairs smaller than 20 square feet, are exempt. Housing for the elderly and disabled (unless a child younger than 6 lives or will live there) and zero-bedroom dwellings such as efficiency apartments are also exempted from the rule.

At this time, do-it-yourselfers also have an out. The EPA rule applies only to renovations performed by businesses for compensation (which includes landlording). Still, the agency recommends that homeowners follow the procedures.

Handling security deposits

Know the maximum security deposit allowed in your state and collect it. We are allowed to collect two months' rent as a security deposit. Most residents will forfeit all or at least part of their deposit when they move. The No. 1 reason for forfeiture is failure to give a thirty-day notice to vacate. The more money the tenant puts down to move in, the better this person will care for your property in the hopes of getting this deposit back at move out. And, if a tenant leaves owing you for rent or damage, this deposit provides the means to recover your losses.

Warning: Tenant deposit money may not be co-mingled with any of your own money. It is not yours. This deposit money is the tenant's money until such time as they move out and all or part of it becomes yours to cover unpaid amounts and/or repairs. Until that time, you may not touch it; you may not spend it. Failure to place deposit money in the appropriate account can be cause for lawsuit against you.

The security deposit belongs to the tenant, not to the landlord, until such time as they move out and all or part of it becomes yours to cover unpaid amounts and/or repairs.

This, like many landlord/tenant policies, is state specific. In many states, you must hold all tenant deposits in a federally insured bank in an escrow account, a separate account used only for that purpose. In some states, you may post a bond rather than collecting and holding the deposit in an escrow account.

Some states allow you to have an interest-bearing escrow account and keep the earned interest. In some states, the interest belongs to the tenant. Some states require non-interest bearing bank accounts for collected deposits.

Know your state's requirements.

Chapter 12

BASIC LANDLORDING QUESTIONS

Because we handle so many properties, and because we coach and train others to own rental properties, we receive a lot of landlording questions. I wrote down some of the most commonly asked ones here.

1. **Should I charge an application fee when prospects apply to rent a property?**

   Yes, if they want to fill out your application, they pay the application fee. The fee pays for your time, or your employees' time, to verify what they put on the application. Also, you will pay to check their credit and to do a criminal background check. That cost should be covered by what they give you for their application fee.

2. **When sending out the rental application to a prospect, should I also send the rental/lease contract so they can review it and know what they will be signing if they rent the house?**

No, you'll overwhelm them with details they don't care about yet. Wait until they've had a chance to see the house and fall in love with it. Don't put too much information in their way this early on.

3. **I worry about someone willing to sign the rental/lease contract without reading it first.**

Most people never read it. Ask homeowners if they've ever read the documents they signed when purchasing their home. If they want the house, most care only whether they can afford it.

We as landlords, however, take the details very seriously. When a prospect plans to move into one of our properties, we have them allow sixty minutes for their "signing ceremony" (hopefully they've left the children at home). At that time, we read over the contract with them line-by-line and have them initial the main items as well as the bottom of every page.

Read over the contract with your tenant line-by-line and have them initial the main items as well as the bottom of every page.

Many tenants get antsy and just want to sign and leave. We make sure to go over, at the very least, the details of rental amount, any available rental discounts, any charges such as late fees and bounced check fees, pet fees (even if they don't have a pet), repair responsibilities, and move-out information.

We then have them sign those line items indicating they have been explained and understood.

4. **What is normally charged for pet fees?**

I don't know that there is a "normal." Check to see if your state has laws regulating these fees. We charge a $250 non-refundable pet deposit, more for multiple pets. Yes, even adorable Fluffy will cause damage. In addition, many also charge $15 to $25 per-month per pet pet rent. Tenants love Fluffy and know she is worth it. The pet rents are negotiable as needed: for example, $25 per month pet rent for two cats rather than $15 per month each. You will spend additional money on repairs when pet owners move out, so it is reasonable to ask them to pay additional fees for their pets.

5. **What kind of background/credit check do you recommend?**

There are many online sources for checking criminal background, past rental behavior, and credit. National Tenant Network is a great resource and you can check them out at NTNonline.com. Research multiple online services, depending upon what you want to check, and notice that fees do vary.

6. **What criteria do you go by in selecting a tenant?**

Prospects must have a good job history and an income that will allow them to afford the property for which they are applying. Employment history and income are the first things we consider. If a prospect has a good job, makes good money, and can pay the required down payment with the first month's rent, this person is good.

Employment history and income are the first things we consider in tenant screening.

Prospects must be employed (no, we do not count unemployment as income), and we do call their employers and previous landlords to verify their applications and behaviors.

In addition, we run a criminal background and credit history check. If they aren't paying their other bills on a consistent basis, the same pattern will emerge with their rent. If they show a history of skipping out on landlords, chances are they'll do the same to you. Because so much of this can be found online, do the search. And, when a tenant is a problem and/or moves out without paying you, be sure to add that to their online background information for the next potential landlord to find.

7. **Can I sell my property with a residing tenant?**

If you buy or sell a property with tenants already in it, they are allowed, by law, to remain until their rental contract expires.

Yes, you can. However, the tenant lease gives your tenants protection in that the lease is good until the expiration date. If you sell a property with tenants already in it, they are allowed, by law, to remain until their rental contract expires. The tenant, their contract, and their security deposit transfer from you to the new owner at the time of sale.

Chapter 13

INFORMATION TO PROVIDE FOR YOUR TENANT

Since the housing meltdown, nearly 3 million new households have become renters. At least 3 million more are expected by 2015. Rentals are on the rise! Many current-day tenants are new to the rental market so don't be surprised when you get a lot of questions from these first-time renters. Here are some common questions you'll hear before they sign your contract.

> *Many current-day tenants are new to the rental market so don't be surprised when you get a lot of questions from these first-time renters.*

Answers you need for new tenants

1. How much is the application fee?
2. What documents do you require when I submit my application?
3. Will you run a credit check?
4. Will you run a criminal background check?
5. How much is the security deposit?
6. Which fees are nonrefundable?
7. How long is the term of the lease or rental agreement?
8. What are the extra charges for pets?
9. How do I pay rent? (check, money order, credit card—we prefer no cash)
10. What day of the month is rent due?
11. What day of the month do late fees begin accruing?
12. If I move in after the first of the month, will I be charged for the entire month?
13. Can I paint any rooms of the property?
14. Can I install a security system?
15. Is the property all electric? If not, which items are gas?
16. What are the names, addresses, and phone numbers of the utility companies for this property?
17. How are maintenance requests handled?
18. Are there smoke and carbon monoxide detectors installed in this property?

19. How much will rent increase each year?

20. Am I allowed to sub-let?

21. Can I add someone to the lease at a later date?

22. Can I rent month-to-month? Is there an additional fee?

23. If my lease ends, does it automatically revert to month-to-month or must I sign a new lease?

24. What is the fee if I terminate the lease early?

25. When and how do I get my security deposit back?

These are all things you need to think through and decide on before you begin marketing. Some items are designated by state or federal law (i.e., 5, 18, 25), but most of the rest are left to your discretion. Just be sure to decide ahead of time, and don't discriminate—the law for one is the law for all.

Things tenants look for:

- Tenants don't just check out the property, they also check out the landlord to make sure they're renting/leasing from someone who's reputable. At least they should.
- They want to see if you have a website.
- They will check to see if the rent you're requesting is reasonable. Get an idea by checking rentrange.com.
- Many will check crime in the area through various crime check sites such as CrimeReports.com.
- To get an idea of utility costs before they sign a contract, prospects can call the city water, gas, and electric companies. Most utility companies will provide a six to twelve month average for the address.

Things you need to do:

- **Provide legal contracts.**

  Obtain forms from, or take the ones you are currently using to, an attorney to make sure they are federal and state compliant. I prefer to have my contracts looked over by an attorney who is also willing to defend them in a court of law, should that be necessary.

  I prefer to have my contracts looked over by an attorney who is also willing to defend them in a court of law, should that be necessary.

  Spell out, in your contracts, all of your leasing rules and regulations. Take time to go over them, in detail, with anyone who will be signing them. Have them initialed, signed, and dated by all tenants 18 years of age and older, who will be living in your property.

- **Provide disclosures.**

  For example, federal law requires landlords to provide a lead-based paint pamphlet and a signed disclosure as part of the lease agreement for all houses built before 1978.

- **Provide tenants, as part of the rental agreement, information on what qualifies as an emergency and what qualifies as something the tenant needs to take care of.**

  Important criteria for this involves safety of the tenants and potential damage to the property.

  This is a good place to suggest to the tenants that they obtain their own rental insurance. We not only suggest it, we provide the name of a source for renters insurance and request a copy of the tenant's policy rider once their insurance has been purchased. An owner's landlord policy covers the structure, but not the contents as the contents belong to the tenant. The tenant, therefore, needs to obtain their own renter's insurance which will cover the contents only (their possessions) but not the structure. Renter's insurance is very inexpensive.

- **Know the laws and regulations for leases in the state your rentals are in.**

This should be obvious. Not every state has the same laws for leasing. These laws are in place to protect both the tenant and the landlord. Know them, so you don't have to find out what they are in court. "I wasn't aware" will not help you in a court of law.

Chapter 14

FORMS AND CONTRACTS

Following are a few of the forms and contracts I've used in my landlording business. Feel free to use them, but be sure to modify them to your specifications and state requirements.

Application Process

Thank you for your interest in our property. Our staff will do everything possible to assist you in this process. Please begin by completing and returning the resident application.

1. **Each adult over 18** planning to occupy the property must fill out an application and an authorization form allowing (company name) to perform a credit check and criminal background check.

2. There is a $__________ **nonrefundable application fee for each applicant** payable at the time the application is turned in. Payment must be in CERTIFIED FUNDS or credit card. No checks or cash will be accepted for application fee.

3. You will need to have the following information for each filled out application:

   - **Valid, Legible Driver's License or Picture Identification Card and**

   - **Legible Social Security Card and**

   - **Most Recent Pay Stubs.** (If you are self-employed, we will need two years tax returns and will make a copy of them for our records.)

4. **Once your application is received** your information will be processed. You will be notified as to whether you have been approved within 48 business hours. During this time, we will run your credit report, perform a criminal background check, verify current employment, and check your credit references. If you are approved for the property, you will be asked to pay a security deposit and first month's rent. No properties will be taken off the market until we receive payment for them in full.

5. **Pet Deposit** (if applicable)—There is a nonrefundable $__________ pet fee for up to two (2) pets living at the

address for *any* length of time. The pet fee is $_________ for three (3) pets. In addition, there is a $____.00/mo. charge for each pet over 25 pounds and a $_____/mo. charge for any pet under 25 pounds. Maximum number of pets allowed is ________.

6. **All initial payments**—application fee, deposits, pet fees, and first month's rent, must be paid in CERTIFIED FUNDS or credit card. No checks or cash will be accepted for application fee, deposits, fees, or first month's rent.

7. **Once you have completed your application**:

   Fax it to: (fax number) ______________________________

   E-mail it to: (e-mail) ______________________________

   or Drop it off at our office: (address) __________________

   ____

8. **Feel free to contact us** with additional questions: (phone#) ____________________

Rent Payment Policies

1. We accept NO CASH for payments of any kind. All payments are to be made by check, certified funds, bank transfers, or credit card. If you come to the office with cash, you will be directed to a nearby bank to purchase a money order.

2. NO CHECKS will be accepted for late payments. ALL payments and late fees made after the 5th (fifth) day of ANY month MUST be paid in certified funds ONLY. Any checks received after the 5th of the month will be returned to you and eviction proceedings will continue.

3. Court Filing Fee - On the _____ day of every month, if we have not received your payment, eviction proceedings commence. At that time, _____% of your rent will be added to your monies owed as a late fee. A court filing fee will also be added to your outstanding balance.

4. Once eviction proceedings have commenced, they may be stopped only with payment from you in full including past due rents, late fees, court costs, and all unpaid balances on your account. Again, all such monies must be presented to us in CERTIFIED FUNDS ONLY. No checks, credit cards, or cash will be accepted.

5. All payments must be made out to: ________________.

6. Monthly rent/lease payments should be mailed to us by the 25th so they are received in our office no later than the first of the month. Payments not in our office or mailbox by 5:00 p.m. on the 5th of the month are LATE and late fees will be applied to your account.

Our office has done everything it can to keep costs down to prevent rent increases. The above policies are necessary to (1) help you toward your goal of enjoying a home (2) keep down our costs of rent collection.

We appreciate your efforts, your tenancy, and your attention to the above details.

Sincerely,

Resident's General Utility and Property Information

Property Address: ______________________________

Schools: ______________________________

Following is a list of some telephone numbers/information that might be helpful.

Utilities:	Name:	Phone Number:
Electric	Name of electric company	800-555-1212
Gas	Name of gas company	800-555-1212
Water	Name of water company	800-555-1212

Trash pick-up on ______________

Rent payments payable to: ______________________

Mail to: ______________________

____

Phone: ______________________

Fax: ______________________

E-mail: ______________________

To ensure we receive your payment on time, please mail check by the 25th of the month. A warrant for dispossessory will be filed on the 5th of the month if your rent payment has not been received.

Consistent with your rental agreement, there will be a $__________ service charge for any check returned for insufficient funds. In addition, management will only accept rental payment in the form of certified checks or money orders thereafter.

We look forward to your tenancy, we appreciate your business, and

Welcome to Your New Home!

Reminder of Late Payment

NO OTHER NOTICE WILL BE GIVEN

Date ______________________________

Tenant Name ______________________________

Tenant Address ______________________________

____

You are hereby notified that your rent is now past due and payable for the premises held and occupied by you. Your account is now delinquent in the amount of your monthly rent of $______________ plus the ______ % late fee of $______________. An additional court filing fee will be added when we file your eviction. The total amount due and payable from you is now $ ______________________.

These monies are due immediately and must be paid in full in CERTIFIED FUNDS ONLY.

Legal proceedings will be instituted against you to recover possession of said premises, to declare the forfeiture of the Lease or Rental Agreement under which you occupy said premises, and to recover rents and damages, together with court costs and attorney's fees, according to the terms of your Lease or Rental Agreement. Acceptance of your rent after the due date shall not alter the terms of your rental agreement.

Making timely payments is of great importance, and your payment must be received in our office by 5:00 p.m. on the payment due date in order to be on time.

If you have already sent your payment to us, it will be returned unless not paid in full and in certified funds. If you have questions, contact us at ____________________.

Thank you for your immediate attention to this matter.

______________________________, Property Manager

Notice of Intent to Vacate

Date ______________________________

Name ______________________________

Address ______________________________

____

As TENANT of the above-referenced PREMISES, you are hereby notified that I/We have elected not to renew the lease of the PREMISES and will vacate on, or before, the following date:______________ ________, ________

Month Day Year

Accordingly, TENANT is further notified that:

1. TENANT must vacate the PREMISES on or before said lease expiration date.
2. If TENANT does not vacate the premises on or before said lease expiration date, the Lease payment amount will double from the current lease rate.
3. All rent must be timely paid. The security deposit is not a substitute for the last month's rent or any other month's rent.
4. All keys, garage door openers, and other items related to the PREMISES must be returned to ______________(address) immediately upon vacating the PREMISES. TENANT will be charged for additional days after lease termination until items are returned.
5. Lease termination is not permitted on any day other than the last day of the month.

Thank you,

Tenant: (Print Name)______________________________

Date______________________________

Signature______________________________

Tenant: (Print Name)______________________________

Date______________________________

Signature______________________________

Move Out Requirements

(Company Name)

(Company Address)

Date ______________________________

____

____

____

Re: Move Out Requirement of Rental Agreement

Dear ____________________:

The Rental Agreement we entered into has several provisions, which you agreed to, regarding completion of our Agreement. We find that our residents appreciate being reminded of these requirements prior to move out so they can leave on good terms and receive good references. Most of our residents who follow these move-out instructions receive their full deposit refund.

Based on your Rental Agreement, you have agreed as follows:

(a) Lease term has expired or agreement has been terminated by both parties; and

(b) All monies due Management by Resident have been paid; and

(c) Property is not damaged and is left in its original condition, normal wear and tear excepted.

(d) Carpets, walls, floors, appliances, bathroom fixtures, and other areas of the house have been cleaned and are ready for the new Resident. Resident shall provide proof that the carpets were professionally cleaned; and professionally treated for ticks and fleas, if detected or if pets were present.

(e) Yard and shrubbery are neatly trimmed and leaves, trash and other debris have been removed from premises.

(f) Written notice to vacate has been given Management at least 60 days prior to vacating.

(g) Resident allows Management to show premises and post sign during 60-day notice period.

(h) Resident has returned all keys to Management.

(i) Resident has given Management his/her forwarding address.

(j) Resident has paid all final bills on all utilities that have been his/her responsibility under this Agreement.

For your convenience we've enclosed a Move-Out Cleaning Instructions Checklist. We appreciate your cooperation with the Agreement. Please contact us when you are ready to make arrangements for the required move out inspection and to turn in your keys and garage door openers.

Sincerely,

______________________________, Property Manager

Chapter 15

THE MOVE-IN PACKET

We create a move-in packet for every new tenant and I suggest you do the same. This packet contains all the forms and contracts they signed to move into your property as well as all the rules and regulations for living there in one convenient, orderly bundle.

Don't forget, every person you sign up is immediately going to be packing all their belongings and moving to a new home. Be sure your documents are together in one easy-to-find packet that they will be able to store and retrieve as needed.

The move-in packet contains all the forms and contracts they signed to move into your property as well as all the rules and regulations for living there in one convenient, orderly bundle.

What's in a tenant move-in packet?

You can create your own system but, to give you a guideline, here's what ours include:

1. **Rental agreement**—This is the tenant's copy of the complete, signed, dated rental agreement.
2. **Lead-based paint brochure**—Must be given to tenants moving into any property built in 1978 or before.
3. **Utility information sheet**—This includes the tenant's new address and all names, addresses, and phone numbers of the utility providers for that address. It's great, if you have it, to include local school names and addresses on this sheet as well.
4. **Our resident handbook**—This is a brochure we have created that reiterates much of the information we go over with them at the rental contract signing. It is a handbook for them to reference when they have questions about our policies on everything involving the tenant, including online payments and how to submit repair requests.
5. **Property manager's business card**—This is another place they can find our contact information, if needed.
6. **Move-in/move-out checklist**—We create three copies. The first copy shows the move-in condition of the property as we know it. We keep one in their tenant file in our office and put a copy of this same checklist in their packet for them to take. These are both filled out completely by us, showing them everything we are aware of that is wrong in every room (or noting fresh paint, new/shampooed carpets, etc.). They sign and date both their copy and ours. We also include a blank copy in their packet and tell them to fill it out and mail it back to us within two weeks, marking any flaws they find in the house once they've moved in. This does not mean we will correct any items they record; it simply shows us what is there upon move-in so they will not be charged for it when

they move out. If they do not mail this sheet back to us, both parties agree that our original copy was correct. This form, signed and dated by all parties involved, will save a lot of confusion and argument when they move out and try to blame you for a problem by saying "that was there when we moved in"—not if it wasn't recorded on the signed move-in sheet!

7. **Coupons to local merchants**—It's ideal to include discount items for things that will help them take care of your home, such as yard maintenance and carpet cleaning.

We also include a copy of our book, *The Essential Handbook for Buying a Home*, as our goal is to help them, at some point, be able to buy a home. This is a great book for you to hand out to your clients, as well. Be sure to include something extra that makes you stand out from other landlords in the area. This initial contact is when you and your client begin building a lasting relationship.

It's ideal to include discount items for things that will help them take care of your home, such as yard maintenance and carpet cleaning.

We present everything to them in a large manila envelope with their new address and all of our contact information listed on the outside. I encourage our new residents to put this envelope in a location where they can easily access it before, during, and after their move.

It's a nice touch to include a special move-in gift as they're ready to leave your office with their move-in packet completed. Secure a double-pack of toilet paper together with a roll of paper towels and tie together with a bow (two things everyone needs in a new home). Give them a small potted plant. Hand them a gift certificate for a delivered pizza and tell them it's your gift for their move-in night. Or tickets to a local movie theater to welcome them to the area.

Be creative. Use your imagination. Send them off feeling excited about you and their new home.

Section Four

THE MONEY

The money, after all, is why most people want to be landlords. Profit, right? But before we get profit, we have to acquire a property, prepare it, market it, screen a tenant, and collect this tenant's money every single month.

Now that you've gotten your property and a qualified prospect, let's turn them into a tenant and start collecting the money.

Chapter 16

RENT COLLECTION

If you have a problem with this area of your business, you're out of business.

Collecting rent is possibly *the* most important aspect of landlording. It is definitely the most mentally stressing part of your relationship with your tenants. Maintenance issues happen occasionally - rent collection happens every single month.

Without rent collection, you can't pay your bills, maintain your properties, or enjoy any profit!

When do we discuss the rent collection policy?

Immediately. Discuss your rent collection policy in detail at the time of contract signing. Rent collection is one of the most important aspects of tenancy so you want to ensure that everyone is on the same page about it. Be sure to go over rent collection in GREAT DETAIL when you sign the contracts.

Discuss your rent collection policy in detail at the time of contract signing.

Our contracts start with the date, resident name, management name, property address, beginning and ending date of contract, then rental amount and collection procedures.

What does "on time" mean?

You definitely want to discuss when rent is expected and what the consequences are if it is late. On time typically means in your office by 5:00 p.m. the day it is due. It never matters when the payment was mailed; it matters when it is received. If the due date falls on the weekend, payment needs to be in your possession by 5:00 p.m. the Friday before (even if it will not be deposited until the following Monday) or it is late. Payment on Monday because rent was due the day before and "you were closed" is not an accepted excuse. Payment is DUE no later than 5:00 p.m. on the DUE DATE, no matter which day of the week or holiday it falls on.

One way to deal with late payments is to charge a late fee for payments that do not arrive by the due date. Check to find how much late fee can be added and the date you can add it. These regulations are state specific, not nationally regulated.

Payment method

The preferred method of payment is direct deposit, payroll deduction, or debit card collection. Mailing checks is fine. I encourage tenants to mail their payments on the 25th so we have them by the first. What you DO NOT want is for the tenant to come into the office to make their payment. This is time consuming, disruptive to the person who must stop to collect the payment and create a receipt, and encourages too much unneeded activity and conversation in the office. Of course if this happens, we are thrilled to take the payment, we just want to streamline our processes and make payment fast and efficient for everyone involved.

No cash

No, don't take cash, ever.

I know it sounds like a good idea, and who doesn't like a handful of cash? However, not in business. Why? First, you don't want people to think you have cash in the office or on your person, so don't. This is simply a much safer way to do business. No one wants to walk out at the end of the day with a bag full of cash to take to the bank. This creates unnecessary opportunity for crime and theft.

Second, you won't want the hassle of trying to make change for people. It's rare for anyone to have the exact amount.

Finally, with cash, there is no way to track client payments or to prove their payment history. If your client, at any time, decides to purchase the property (see Chapter 10—Lease with Option to Buy), banks do not accept photocopies of cash as proof of payment. Nor will they accept copies of your written receipts. What they will accept are copies of checks, money orders, or bank checks.

If someone shows up at our office with cash, we are conveniently located on a busy intersection with three banks, a drug store, and a grocery store within walking distance. We send them off to purchase a money order. Your location may not be so convenient and, as hard as it is to send someone away who is holding cash, you only have to do this once or twice before they learn to purchase the money order before coming to you.

Never worry about late payments again!

Every landlord wants on-time payments and, believe it or not, your tenants would prefer to pay on-time so they don't have to think about it or pay late fees.

Help them out by offering the option to pay rent automatically each month. It's fast, easy, hassle free, and they'll never have to worry about late payments again. To implement, simply ask at contract signing which checking account they will be using during the term of their rental. Request permission to draft that account on agreed-to dates each month. Bank procedures vary. Some will require you, the landlord, to

Help them out by offering the option to pay rent automatically each month.

set up the auto-draft; some will require their client, your tenant, to set it up. Contact your bank and learn the process; you'll be glad you did.

Have more than one payment option available

It's always best to have more than one "standard" payment method. We collect automatic payments either by check draft or electronic transfer. We tell our tenants, *"We do the work so you don't have to."* Let your residents know that they never have to worry about mailing in their payments or being hit with a late fee. You may even wish to offer a "lower" rental rate, a year-end "discount," or a "rebate" if they select one of these automatic methods of payment.

When explaining the options, let potential tenants know that auto-pay is your standard operating procedure and focus on the ease and convenience for them. Let them know that setting up these payment options is free to them!

These methods work especially well, and may be required, if a third party will be making the payment for your resident. For example, parents of college students know that you have received the payment when it goes directly to your account rather than into their child's.

You should also implement these policies with existing tenants. Let everyone know these options are available and are, going forward, the preferred procedure. In addition, after two late payments or a bounced check, insist on these methods to avoid further late fees and eviction.

Payment options

1. An **electronic fund transfer** (EFT) transfers funds electronically from the resident's checking account to yours. These direct rent deposits are automatic and eliminate the need for paper checks. Also referred to as **ACH payments**,

these deposits occur through the Automated Clearing House payment network.

EFT payments require only a one-time setup where the resident provides his/her checking account information. It can be as simple as submitting a voided check to you. The process is then set-up and handled by the bank.

You are not able to withdraw more than the agreed to amount. Residents are protected by Federal Regulation E—the Electronic Funds Transfer Act of 1978—against "inappropriate movement of funds" from their account.

The resident is responsible to maintain adequate funds in the checking account to cover rent each month or, just as with a bounced check, you will receive an insufficient funds notice. You will, however, find out much sooner with ACH payments than with the traditional check writing method.

2. With **pre-authorized paper check drafts**, your customer's check is created by the bank on the appropriate day each month and mailed for deposit into your bank. It is handled and deposited exactly like a paper check that the customer has written himself or herself. The payment is not withdrawn from the customer's bank account until you deposit the check. With check drafts, there is no computer access into your customer's checking account.

3. **Direct deposits.** Have tenants make direct deposits to your bank rather than coming to your office. Give them your bank name, the name on the account (which should be your business, not your personal name), and your account number. They have authority to make deposits and no other access to the account. They e-mail confirmation to you that payment has been made; you verify online. Their bank receipt is proof of deposit if there is ever a dispute.

4. **Credit or debit cards.** Banks charge a fee when you accept credit or debit cards so you may choose to pass this fee on to your clients. If not, be sure to figure this fee into your costs.

5. **Checks**. While not preferred, checks are also acceptable as a form of payment.

So what's wrong with checks?

Yes, we accept checks, just not cash. So what's wrong with checks? First of all, you wait in the hopes that they arrive. We've all heard the dreaded, "the check is in the mail," where we're left to wait in great anticipation. There are occasions, however, when they never arrive.

Once you receive the check, you must enter the payment into your system, whatever that is, create a deposit slip, and make a trip to the bank. We also make a photocopy of the check and place it in the tenant's file. All of this is time consuming and, whether you do it yourself or pay a staff person to do it, it ends up being costly.

How long do you wait for the check to arrive before you realize it's not coming? Days, sometimes weeks later, you may discover that it bounced. Then what? You're way behind on your payment and need to (1) contact the tenant and wait for their make-up payment—certified funds only at this point—and (2) begin the eviction process before they get any further behind and you lose more time and money.

Certainly not all checks are bad and we are thrilled to get the good ones.

Certainly not all checks are bad and we are thrilled to get the good ones, deposit them, and pay our bills. It's just not the fastest or most secure form of payment.

On-time payment incentives

On-time payments make life easier for you as the landlord as well as for the tenant. Your tenant is building a good habit of paying on time and a good record that will follow him or her to a new rental and to a home that he or she buys in the future. Landlords can help encourage this healthy habit by offering an

Some feel that offering a reward rather than the threat of a penalty can be a great motivator.

incentive, often in the form of discounted rent for timely payments.

The way most landlords handle a discounted rent is by advertising the "discounted" price. "Full" rent includes an additional $20 or more added in. Savings can be whatever you decide, typically 10 percent. For example, if you want $1,000 for rent payment, you advertise it for $1,000. Your contract reads that rent is $1,100 but will be discounted to $1,000 if paid on or before the first. If payment is made after the first, however, it goes up to the "full" rental amount of $1,100.

Some feel that offering a reward rather than the threat of a penalty can be a great motivator.

Double check with your state laws to see if offering rental discounts is permitted. As with late payments, these regulations are specific to each state.

Payment reminders

We mail out an invoice to all residents every month five to seven days before their rent is due. These invoices show what they owe and include all outstanding balances. Late fees accrue each month until all fees are paid. Check your state regulations to see if you can add monthly late fees when your resident has outstanding past dues. Some states allow late fees to be applied only to the current month's rental payment.

If you decide to invoice your clients, show the amount due, the date due, the amount of late fees, and the date late fees are applied. You may want to use a two-part invoice so the resident can keep a copy and return one copy with their payment.

Some landlords send out self-addressed stamped envelopes as an incentive to receive checks on time and at the correct address. I have found that most of my self-addressed stamped envelopes never show up in my mailbox.

Bounced check fees

Check your state regulations to find out the maximum you can charge for any bounced check you receive. We have a very strict policy that, after a bounced check, the resident must make all future payments by bank check or money order.

Chapter 17

LATE PAYMENTS

I'm not sure why anyone would let tenants get behind in their payments without taking action, but I regularly get calls asking what a landlord should do because it's the middle of the month and they still haven't received the payment that was due on the first.

"They said they were going to pay"

"Why haven't you done anything sooner?" I ask. "Well, they said they were going to pay," is the common response.

What other creditor does that line work with? The mortgage company? The gas company? Cable? Where do people learn this tactic? Apparently, from landlords who let them slide rather than responding when the payment is first late.

Have a policy and use it

We have a set policy and we stick to it. Payments are due on the first and late fees start after the fifth. Your tenant is *in breach of contract* after the first. To be clear, payments are late after the first but our state government allows tenants five additional days before late fees apply, so I wait until the sixth to respond to non-pays. Because of this, some tenants don't believe that their rent is due until the fifth and wonder why I'm upset when they want to pay after that. "I'm not even late, yet," is their rationale. However, according to the agreement the tenant signed, rent payment was due on the first, so it is very late on the fifth.

File paperwork with the courts as soon as you can

On the sixth, we can and do file for possession in our clerk of court office. At this time, we add late fees along with ALL legal fees and demand possession of the property for breach of contract. Why? Because I don't want to get to the 20th when they still haven't paid to start my actions. By that time, they may decide to hang out to see how long it will take me to evict and figure it's cheaper to move than to pay me the rent that is due, by then grown to two months' worth. I don't want to give tenants that much time to build up debt or to plan alternatives.

It doesn't help tenants at all to let them get further in debt. The deeper the debt, the harder the recovery.

It doesn't help tenants at all to let them get further in debt. The deeper the debt, the harder the recovery. In fact, it's just enabling poor habits that won't help them anywhere in life. And, it definitely doesn't help you or get the mortgage paid, which is, for you as the owner of the property, the bottom line. If you can't pay the mortgage, you lose the house and your income, and the tenant loses a place to live.

Explain your eviction policies before they move in

I begin every tenant relationship in the same way, by letting them know the rules of conduct that are expected, beginning with on-time payments. I let them know the consequences if payments are not on time—court proceedings and added fees on top of their regular payment. These are not fees I'm adding; these are fees they're creating for themselves by not abiding by the terms of the contract. My end of the bargain is to provide the housing they live in, which I've done. Their end of the bargain is to pay the agreed to amount on the first of the month. I see no confusion in that arrangement.

As a landlord, you can report to all three major credit bureaus and to online rental screening services the non-payments and late payments. In fact, you should as a warning to future landlords and creditors. If you plan to do this, be sure to let your tenants know in advance that this is your policy.

These are not fees I'm adding; these are fees they're creating for themselves by not abiding by the terms of the contract.

Sending late notices

Save yourself time and money. No need to send repeated late notices. They know they're late. We send a "pay or quit" and let them know that we have filed at the courthouse on the 6th of the month. They must now come in and pay their rent, late fees, and court filing fees in order to stop the eviction process. If they don't want to move, doing this once or twice usually ends the bad habit. If they don't intend to pay, we have nipped it quickly and don't lose more than one month's rent.

Be sure to know the eviction laws in your state. In some states, the process is more difficult and time consuming. Typically, late is three, five, seven, or ten days before you can start the legal eviction process. Whatever it is, don't delay. Let your tenants to know, without a doubt, what your actions will be if rent is not paid as agreed.

Working with the tenant

If you have not dealt with tenants before, your first instinct will tell you to be understanding and work out a catch-up plan

The first few months of tenancy is the most critical time to begin the habit of swift enforcement.

for them because, after all, there was a sickness/illness/death/flat tire/paycheck mishap/etc., and you can understand how this can happen. Stop yourself. Take it from someone who's heard all the stories and has tried everything to be the "good guy"—it's a business. Payment is due from the tenant just like mortgage payments are due from the landlord. I'm sorry about their life issues getting in the way of their paycheck, but you can't let their life issues get in the way of yours.

However, be reasonable and be responsible. If the resident has a good record of on-time payments but an out-of-the-ordinary problem arises, naturally you should work with this person. A good tenant is one you want to keep. A good tenant will be late only once a year (and have a very good reason).

The first few months of tenancy is the most critical time to begin the habit of swift enforcement. Once they recognize you are not a slack landlord but that you say what you mean and mean what you say, you should have a smooth relationship and on-time payments.

Chapter 18

EXTRA FEES AND CHARGES

Besides rent, there are other ways to make money on a rental property.

Additional Income Streams:

1. Rent detached garages separately to either the tenant or to someone else as storage space. My sister is a landlord in Sydney, Australia, where parking spaces are hard to come by. She has a detached double garage with one of her rental units. The people in the unit rent one side of the garage; someone else rents the other side.

2. Rent appliances such as washers, dryers, refrigerators, or lawn mowers to your residents. Many tenants need and want these items but don't have the credit to go out and buy them. You can purchase the items and then rent them to your resident. Consider a cash deposit that is refundable when they move out and the appliance is left in good working order.

3. You can also buy new or used appliances and sell them over time, with interest, to your residents instead of renting

them. Use a Promissory Note or binding contract that is recorded or held by your attorney to be sure you receive payment and to have a legal claim if you don't.

4. Provide cable or Internet if residents cannot qualify to get it on their own.

5. Charge to replace lost keys or to let in a resident who has locked himself or herself out of the property.

6. Charge for any service you need to provide after hours.

7. Charge for any extra service you can provide. For example, some residents won't want to keep up their own lawns. You can offer lawn maintenance for a fee.

8. If you need extra cash today, offer a rental discount if your resident can pay six months, or even a year, in advance.

9. If someone needs a shorter rental agreement, maybe only six or nine months, charge a premium rent. This is a common practice so your potential tenant should expect it.

10. Raise rents when the lease expires, even if you plan to raise them by a lower amount for good residents. As we explain, the need to raise rents is because the property owner's taxes, insurance, and HOA fees tend to go up every year. You can give an incentive for longer rental agreements; i.e., raise rents 5% per year or only 3% per year if they renew for two years.

11. Use the same paint color in all your houses and buy it in large quantities. We use Swiss Coffee Eggshell on the walls and white on the trim and doors. This not only saves money on the materials, but saves time and eliminates the mistake of touching up with the wrong paints or colors.

Use the same paint color in all your houses and buy it in large quantities.

12. Have residents responsible for minor repairs. When signing the rental contracts, assure new tenants that they are responsible for minor issues and list some of them in the contract or in the tenant handbook. For example, if a resident backs up the toilet, we explain that they are responsible to repair this issue as they created it.

Check your state laws

Having listed all of these, I want to stress that you can't, of course, charge for any work or repairs that you, as the landlord, are required by law to repair.

Also, never charge extreme amounts for any of your fees or services. Adding 25 percent to the monthly amount of refrigerator payments is overboard and will get you into trouble.

Even monthly late fees applied to rental payments are regulated. Never charge more than allowed by law.

See what fees and amounts are legal by checking with your state's consumer affairs division.

Section Five

MANAGING PROPERTIES FOR OTHERS

This will be a short section but I want to include some things you'll need to know if you plan to manage properties you don't own. This includes properties owned by friends and family members, by the way. The law is very clear; there is a definite difference between managing a property you own and managing one you don't.

The law is very clear; there is a definite difference between managing a property you own and managing one you don't.

To begin with, if you are managing property for others, you are required to be a licensed real estate agent. Further, a property management agreement between the licensed broker and the property owner must be in writing from the outset of the relationship, prior to the broker providing any services.

Unlicensed property owners may NOT pay unlicensed persons who have no ownership interest in the property to assist them in leasing or managing property they own, even if such persons are related to the property owner.

So, while it's fine for anyone to manage their own properties, both federal and state laws strictly govern anyone managing properties owned by others.

Chapter 19

COMMON QUESTIONS IF YOU MANAGE FOR OTHERS

As a property management company, we find that some questions come up quite frequently. If you plan to manage for others, here are some questions you should be prepared to answer:

Q. Why shouldn't I manage my property myself?

A. You absolutely can manage yourself. However, you are emotionally attached and that does not always make for the best landlord/tenant relationship. You may be more protective and defensive than you need to be. Unless, of course, you can detach and remember that the property is an income vehicle and all you need to be concerned with are the numbers, not the scratches and dents.

There is a danger that you will take the behavior and attitude of your tenants personally, and you just can't as a landlord. What they do is not a reflection on you, it's a reflection on them, but when it's your money on the line, defensiveness can come in like a wave.

Some important questions to consider: Do you have the time available? Landlording will interfere with your nights, weekends, and vacation time. It will also interfere with your normal 40-hour workweek. Landlording is not something you do in your spare time, but requires your attention at a moments notice. Do you know how to market your property to find tenants? Are you familiar with doing your own tenant screenings and background checks? Do you have resources available such as maintenance and repair people on call? Do you know the state and federal laws regarding managing tenants?

Q. What information do you need from me in order to manage my property?

A. We have a contract that will be agreed to and signed by both of us. At time of signing, we also require that you submit the completed forms we sent to you providing us with an itemized list of all your property amenities and utility information.

If you manage a property owned by someone else, you are required to be a licensed real estate agent or to employ a licensed real estate agent who handles the property management responsibilities for you.

Q. Are any licenses required to perform property management?

A. Not to manage properties you own personally. Anyone can manage his or her own properties with no license. If, however, you manage a property owned by someone else, you are required to be a licensed real estate agent or to employ a licensed real estate agent who handles the property management responsibilities for you.

Q. How much does professional property management cost?

A. Fees vary by company. Typically, the initial fee is anywhere from 50 percent to 100 percent of the first month's rent for marketing the property, screening tenants, signing contracts, and moving the tenant in. After that, 10 percent of the monthly rental amount is common. It is possible that you will also be required to keep a minimum amount ($300 to $500) in a property management account so small repairs can be handled quickly.

Q. How do I prepare my property for lease?

A. Have it clean and everything in good working order, just as you would want it if you were moving in.

Q. When will you start advertising my property?

A. As soon as all of the contracts have been signed and the property is vacant, clean, and ready to show.

Q. How do I determine the weekly rent of my property?

A. There are many online sources to find area rents and property comparisons. An example is RentRange.com. We will be happy to discuss with you what we think it should rent for and why.

Q. How do I know you will select a good tenant for my property?

A. We start by having applicants fill out a questionnaire, completely. Next, we do an online tenant screening to check their credit history, criminal background, and past rental performance. They are then rated on a sliding scale—excellent, questionable, absolutely not! Not everything will be found or known about them before we put them into your property, but we do everything we can to make sure they are stable, have a good job history, and can afford the property they're moving into. A bad tenant is time and work for us and we do not want a bad tenant any more than you do.

Q. Are there any charges for property management while my property is vacant?

A. Not monthly, just the same 50 percent of the first month's rent once we find a tenant to help cover our costs for marketing, screening, signing contracts, and moving them in.

Q. What is your policy with late rent payments?

A. We charge a 5 percent late fee (or maximum allowed by law in your state) if they are more than five days late. Always check to see what is allowed where you live. We keep that late fee to cover our expense for chasing and collecting the rent when not paid as agreed.

Q. If I need you only to find a tenant for me, could you do that?

A. Absolutely. The policy to find a tenant is always the same—50 percent of the first month's rent (or whatever it is that you and your company decide to charge). After that, you receive the contracts and the tenant is yours.

Q. What if my tenants break their lease agreement?

A. We follow the process for the laws in our state. After five days, they are accessed a 5 percent late fee in addition to the rental amount. On day seven, they are sent a ten-day notice to pay-or-quit. On day eleven, we go to the courthouse and file the eviction papers.

Q. Can I sell my property with a residing tenant?

A. Yes, you can. However, the tenant lease gives the tenant protection in that the lease is good until the expiration date. If you sell the property with a tenant already in it, they are allowed, by law, to remain until their rental contract expires. The tenant, the contract, and the security deposit would transfer from you to the new owner at the time of sale.

Chapter 20

TAKING OVER A PROPERTY WITH EXISTING TENANTS

Sometimes you may purchase a property that has tenants in it. Sometimes, as a property manager, you may be asked to take over management of a property you do not own that already has tenants in it.

In these cases, what do you need to know?

Their contract stays in effect

Unless a clause is written into the original lease agreement regarding the sale or transfer of the property, the current tenant(s) is/are entitled to live in the property for the term of the original and existing lease. When purchasing a property with an

When purchasing a property with an existing tenant, you must uphold all existing lease agreements.

existing tenant, you must uphold all existing lease agreements as a landlord. The law states that anyone purchasing a unit already occupied by tenants is assumed to have "constructive notice" of the existing lease agreements.

If a tenant is living in the property at the time of sale, the buyer is presumed to have known about the lease arrangement and must abide by this agreement as the new owner. Ultimately, it's the fault of any buyer who failed to investigate the situation and learn about the existing tenants. All existing tenants are entitled to live out their lease.

Does the existing tenant have to sign a new lease

No. Existing tenants never have to sign a new lease agreement with a new landlord. If and when they do, however, sign a new lease agreement, it replaces any former contract and they become bound by the new lease.

What happens to the security deposit

Their original security deposit must be transferred from the previous landlord to the new landlord.

Heads-up! On a property that you purchase, if the old landlord does not transfer the deposit to you, but keeps it, you are still responsible for returning, to the tenant, any deserved portion or all of their deposit at the end of their lease.

On a property that you purchase, if the old landlord does not transfer the deposit to you, but keeps it, you are still responsible for returning, to the tenant, any deserved portion or all of their deposit at the end of their lease.

Previous landlord's responsibilities

The previous landlord or owner should provide the tenant with exact name and contact information of the new landlord, as well as the amount of money transferred to the new landlord.

What happens if the tenants move out

Any tenant you acquire with the purchase of a new property is bound by the terms of the contract they signed when they moved in. They are still obligated to fulfill the contract until it expires and to abide by it as originally agreed.

However, if they wish to move out early, you may choose to allow it with no penalty so that you can put in your own tenant under your preferred terms and with your own contract.

If they wish to move out early, you may choose to allow it with no penalty so that you can put in your own tenant under your preferred terms and with your own contract.

Taking over management of a property you do not own with an existing tenant

If you take over management of a property you do not own and that property has a tenant already in it, the property owner's existing rental agreement between the owner and tenant becomes an assigned contract to you as the new management company and, as the new property manager, you honor (within the law) the agreed-upon terms. At that time, the management company creates an agreement between the property owner and themselves to manage under the current contract terms until expiration. Upon expiration, you can negotiate a new tenant agreement to your own terms, with the owner's permission.

At this point, if the owner does not want to convert to the terms of the new management company, both of you will determine whether or not to continue the relationship.

Section Six

THE EVICTION PROCESS

Sometimes things go awry. It's not always because the tenant was bad; maybe he or she became ill or lost a job.

For whatever reason, things aren't working out and you're no longer collecting rent from the current residents. Let's go through the process of how you move them out so you can move a paying tenant in.

Chapter 21

TENANT EXCUSES: I CAN'T PAY MY RENT BECAUSE . . .

Every month, we hear amazing reasons why our tenants think we should accept them not paying rent. I've considered posting the top excuses and telling tenants not to voice theirs unless they can top those. My problem became limiting the list. Which would you choose?

1. I had a flat tire so I can't pay my rent/can't get to your office.
2. The government hasn't mailed my check yet and I don't know when I'll get it.
3. I just got out of jail so I didn't work last week.
4. I lost my job.
5. My daughter had a baby.
6. My power bill is too high; can you lower my rent?
7. We just bought a new car.

8. They messed up my check at work.

9. The banks are closed by the time I get off work so I can't get your money.

10. How much do you need today?

11. My (insert family member) died and I have to go out of state to the funeral so I won't have time to come by.

12. The check shouldn't have bounced. The money was in my account when I gave it to you.

13. I'm not even really that late.

14. My (fill in the family member) took the money out of my purse/wallet.

15. I had to use the money to fill up my gas tank or I couldn't get to work.

16. I came by last night but you were closed.

17. I mailed it.

18. The church was going to give me the money to catch up but they haven't given it to me yet. (*Shockingly, we've gotten this more than once.*)

19. If I pay you, I can't pay my other bills.

20. We mailed it but I don't think we remembered to put a stamp on it.

21. I will catch up when I get my tax refund (*big excuse November through April*).

22. It was my (fill in the family member's name) birthday and I gave them a party.

23. I don't like to drive in the rain. (*Bummer if you live in Seattle.*)

24. I didn't know it was due again already.

25. How many more days until it's *really* late?

26. I had to use that money for my medicines.

27. My kids just started back to school (*big in the fall*).

28. I have to buy Christmas presents (*December*).

29. I spent too much on Christmas (*January*).

30. The first was on Sunday.

31. I can't drive in the snow.

32. I don't get off work in time.

33. I took my daughter to the mall.

34. My unemployment hasn't started yet.

35. If I pay you, I won't have anything left until payday.

36. I was sick.

37. You made us replace the window we broke so I don't have any money left.

38. We took our kids to the beach for vacation.

39. My son lost his job so I had to pay his rent.

40. I was in a coma. (*Someone actually said this to us so, because it was so unique, I didn't charge him for those three days.*)

41. My ex hasn't sent my child support.

42. I don't know when I'll have time to bring it by.

43. This is all I have. I'll bring more next week.

44. I gave the money order to my friend and they told me they brought it by.

45. I don't have time to go by an ATM machine.

46. You can't evict me for thirty days anyway.

47. The bank messed up my account and now I have to wait until they put the money back in.

48. I mailed your money but I must have mailed it to the wrong place.

49. We'll be able to pay two months' rent next month. (*Of course you will.*)

50. We're going to move. Can we have until the 20th to get out?

Ok, so the point here is, you will hear a lot of excuses. Some better than others.

However, these are the tenant's problems and you don't want them to become yours. Again I'm stressing the importance of sitting down with your tenants when you initially sign the contracts, and go over with them, *in detail,* your policy for late payments and eviction. Excuses are exhausting and don't pay your bills. Do what you can to nip them immediately!

Excuses are exhausting and don't pay your bills.

Chapter 22

THE EVICTION PROCESS

No one likes evictions—not you and not the tenant. But rules are rules. You agreed to provide the property they live in; you did. They agreed to pay each month on a specific date; they did not. This is about as black and white as a contract violation can get, and that's exactly what non-payment is—a contract violation.

You have the law behind you when you go into court over a contract violation such as non-payment of rent. However, the goal of any landlord is to keep the property filled, so it's hard to accept that you need to throw a warm body out of the property.

But if the tenant isn't paying rent, how do *you* pay the mortgage, the taxes, the insurance, and your own bills?

Never delay beginning an eviction

From time to time, tenants won't work out. Some lose jobs and can no longer pay; others turn out to be irresponsible and a problem at the property. No matter what the reason, when you're not receiving rent payments as promised, this is serious and you need to act.

Never delay beginning the eviction process for a number of reasons:

- When you act quickly, the tenant knows you are serious. Some tenants have not had rules enforced before. They need to know that, with you, the rules are to be followed and you will enforce them.

When you're not receiving rent payments as promised, this is serious and you need to act.

- Letting the tenant get behind does not help your tenant. Especially early in your landlording career, you will want to be forgiving and will want to work out solutions for the tenant who has run into some "difficulty" that has prevented on-time or in full payment. Recognize that the further behind the tenant gets, the harder it is to catch up. If a tenant pays fifteen days late, he or she has only fifteen days before the next in full payment is due. What are the odds this tenant will have the full amount again that quickly?

- If you make arrangements to do some sort of work-out with the tenant, document everything and keep the eviction process going in case your tenant doesn't live up to his or her end of the agreement.

- Stop the eviction process only with payment in full (bank check or money order). For example, we explain all the additional fees that will accrue once the process has begun. These include the late fee, court filing fees, and processing fees as allowed by our state for the time and effort we spend in the process. If the tenant wants to stay, he or she may bring all of these monies to us at any time in the eviction process in order to stop the eviction and stay in the property. We never, however, stop the eviction process without payment in full.

- Everyone who signed the lease agreement is considered a responsible party. This is anyone living in the property who is 18 years of age or older. Oftentimes, this also includes co-signers, such as parents of college students. You want all lawsuits, including evictions and attempts to collect past dues, to name every one of those residents.

Keep the communication going

You do have options and I hope this is obvious. If you have a good tenant, you certainly want to work with this person. We manage properties for other people and have hundreds of tenants, so we prefer a "this is the company policy" approach. However, if you have very few properties and own them all yourself, it is much easier to do a more case-by-case operation for eviction.

Consider:

- Problem tenants are the ones you consistently have to chase, month after month, for their rent. It's not as if they don't know they need to make this payment every thirty days.
- It's most important to be strict with the process when a tenant is new. Set the precedent early that you stick to the rules and expect the same from them.
- Communication is vital. When you can't get a hold of the tenant, this is time to act. It's amazing how many times over the years we've been unable to contact a tenant, but when they get a letter from the courts saying the eviction process has begun, we hear from them.

It's not as if they don't know they need to make this payment every thirty days.

- Is an "emergency" truly an emergency situation or an ongoing pattern?

- Will your tenant be able to catch up, or has the situation changed, meaning you need to help them transition to a less expensive property?
- Is the tenant doing as promised, especially when you've agreed to work out late payments? If he or she promises to bring in all past dues including late fees by the 15th, but shows up with only half, it's most likely time for this person to move on. Delaying further will only lead to more frustration for both parties.

Promissory Notes

For past due amounts, you may decide to take payments over time. If so, create a promissory note spelling out amounts due and payment schedule. A promissory note states (1) the tenant owes the money and (2) he or she did not withhold it due to needed repairs or code violations. Creating and signing this note protects you in court because, by signing, your tenant admits to owing it and gives you the legal right to go after the monies owed if payments stop.

Reasons to evict

If a tenant breaks the terms of a rental lease agreement, including failure to pay rent as agreed, or if a tenant poses a health or safety risk to a property and/or other renters at a property, you can lawfully evict.

Past due letters

Mail out past due letters as soon as the rent is late. Sometimes, a tenant only needs a reminder so you want to do this as quickly as possible.

How to begin the eviction process

> *If a tenant breaks the terms of a rental lease agreement, including failure to pay rent as agreed, you can lawfully evict.*

Property owners and managers cannot begin an eviction lawsuit until they terminate the lease by providing written notice to the tenant(s) in question that they are being evicted (see example reminder letter in Chapter 14, Forms and Contracts). Each state has its own laws pertaining what needs to be detailed in this notice, so be sure to check with local government offices to determine what is required to be included in the statement.

Presenting this letter to the tenant(s) prior to beginning the official eviction process is essential because it is written proof you have notified the tenant that you plan to evict and why. Should a renter try to file a discrimination suit against you, you'll need this documentation showing the reason for your decision to file the eviction suit.

Always document all communications with your residents

This is a great time to bring up one of the most important aspects of landlording—keeping good records. Always document all communications with tenants: Make dated copies of any correspondence, and keep these records in the tenant file. In case of confusion (or a court appearance), you never want to depend on "he said, she said." *Keep dated documentation for all communication with every resident.*

When I end any conversation with a tenant, on the phone or in person, I immediately type up a summary of our conversation beginning with, "As per our conversation today." I then go on to outline our discussion. I end by emailing or mailing it to the tenant and putting a copy in their file. This communication makes sure that we agree as to what was discussed and gives me a dated record of all communication.

Always document all communications with tenants: Make dated copies of any correspondence, and keep these records in the tenant file.

Should you go to court, what you don't have doesn't count, so, "I did, your honor, but I don't have the receipt," won't cut it. When your resident complains, "you never told me that," pulling the signed, dated documentation out of the file typically ends all arguments.

I cannot overstate the need to keep detailed records, notes, and copies of all correspondence with your tenants.

You won in court, however . . .

You won in court; however, collecting amounts owed is still up to you. Most of the time, when we go to court, all we care about is regaining possession of our asset, the property. Collecting past-due amounts can be time consuming, costly and, often, fruitless.

Collection agencies exist for a reason. If you win in court, turning your tenant file over to one of these companies may be your best course of action. This prevents you from tying up valuable time and emotional energy where there's very little profit to be made.

What winning does mean is that the process continues. If the tenant still refuses to leave voluntarily, you may need to take the court order to the local sheriff's office and pay a fee for the sheriff to carry out the order.

Personal property left behind

You won the right to possession of your property. However, this does not mean you can go in, remove everything the tenant owns, and put it out on the sidewalk. The law allows tenants a specific period of time to gather their possessions and leave the property.

When tenants leave personal property inside the rental unit after being evicted, some states do not allow landlords to do anything with this property but attempt to contact the prior tenant to get it back to them. Other states allow landlords free rein over abandoned property.

As an example, in our state, if the tenant has left abandoned personal property in the house, we must take our court order to the sheriff to have it enforced. The sheriff then has ten days to enforce it. At sometime during that ten-day period, the sheriff meets us at the property to walk through with us as we make notes of what's been left behind and the property condition. At that time, we are allowed to change the locks. However, we are still not allowed to remove the tenant's property. The tenant then has an additional ten days to retrieve whatever is left. At the end of those ten days, we may remove the property, but we are required to secure it for another thirty days during which the tenant still has the right to come and collect it. At the end of those thirty days, we are finally allowed, by law, to discard any remaining items left by the evicted tenant.

Learn the laws of your state before attempting to handle personal property left behind.

Chapter 23

WHEN YOUR TENANT IS MOVING

Yup, it's gonna happen. So be prepared for it. Tenants move for a lot of reasons: need more space, job transfer, buying a home, loss of a job. Don't take it personally. It's a normal part of the landlording process, but you need to know what to do next when your tenant turns in notice.

The Paperwork

No job is complete until the paperwork is done. As with all other aspects of landlording, a tenant vacating the property comes with its own set.

When your tenant moved in, you went over move-in and move-out requirements in detail at the signing ceremony where these requirements were discussed and agreed to. As this tenant prepares to move out, you should send a written response to the written move-out notice telling your tenant, again, what is expected upon move-out in order to receive their deposit back, in part or in full.

We send the move-out sheet along with a letter stating that we hate to see them go and that "most tenants who follow the enclosed move-out instructions receive their entire deposit back."

Move-out instructions

Be very clear what you expect from the tenant as far as returning the property in the same condition it was when they moved in. This includes getting the carpet professionally cleaned and having the property clean and ready for the next tenant. Send detailed move-out instructions in writing so they know exactly what you will look for on inspection.

Landlord/tenant laws allow for normal wear and tear but not damage.

Landlord/tenant laws allow for normal wear and tear but not damage. Your tenant will be looking for a refund of the deposit and, if he or she doesn't receive all of it, you must be able to document what you're keeping and why.

The next step is to set up a date for the final walk-through inspection of the house.

Final walk-through inspection

When the tenant has finished cleaning up and moving out, schedule a time to meet for a final walk-through and to collect keys and garage door openers.

Take the original move-in sheet with you, the one you filled out and both of you signed and placed in their move-in packet, to note what has changed from the time your tenant moved in.

Returning the security deposit

Most states allow thirty to forty-five days to return the security deposit. Check your state requirements and be sure you conform.

Never give back the deposit at the final walk-through. First of all, you won't know how much to make the check for until you've inspected. Next, there may be things that come up after the tenant has moved that you didn't see right away. There could be unpaid utility bills, and once you give the tenant his or her money back, chances are you won't be able to collect for anything from him or her again. By returning the deposit you have, in fact, agreed that the tenant is entitled to it. By cashing the check, your former tenant has agreed that it is the correct amount due from you.

Never give back the deposit at the final walk-through.

The most effective way to avoid a security deposit dispute is the resident's signature on the move-in inspection sheet that indicates the property was in excellent condition at that time. Some landlords mail a copy of this signed sheet to vacating residents to remind them of the agreed condition when they moved in. This emphasizes that the property needs to be that way again when they move out if they want their deposit back.

Breaking the lease

Not all tenants give a notice. Occasionally, tenants will let you know that they are moving immediately or have already moved. In the worst cases, you drive by to find your property vacant. There are many legitimate reasons a tenant may need to break a lease, such as job transfer or loss of employment. If he or she breaks the contract illegally, two choices are available: (1) attempt court procedures or (2) be happy to have your property back and put in a new tenant.

If your tenant communicates with you and has a legitimate reason, what do you do next?

We always give our tenants the right to find their own replacements if they want to break their lease early. They are allowed to break their lease without penalty if they find a new tenant to move in immediately when they move out.

We have very good success with this. Most people want their full deposit back and, rather than being held to the remaining months of their contract, tenants can move on with no penalty when they put a new tenant in place.

We do not allow sub-leases, however. We want total control of anyone living in our properties, so when residents moves out, the

Give your tenants the right to find their own replacements if they want to break their lease early.

contract is void and a new contract begins with each new tenant.

Encourage your tenants to find a replacement. Offer 100 percent deposit refund, a $50 cash bonus, or reduced move-out fees as an incentive.

Whatever you decide as your policy for breaking a lease, be sure it is clearly spelled out in your rental agreement.

What if they break the lease without a legitimate reason?

All terms of a legally signed lease remain in full force until the lease expiration date. If a tenant moves out before the lease has expired, they are responsible to pay as agreed until the expiration date or until another tenant moves into the property. All fees for damage, late or non-payments, and past due amounts are still due and collectible by you.

If the tenant does not pay these amounts willingly, your next action would be to take them to court or, be thrilled they are gone and you can move in a paying tenant.

When Members of the Military Are Forced to Break Their Lease

If one of your tenants is in the military and is called for active duty, you must release them from their contract obligations without penalty. The Servicemembers Civil Relief Act (SCRA) protects all members of the armed services.

If the rent has been paid in advance, you must return any unearned portion, and you may not withhold the deposit refund. However, you may withhold part or all of the security deposit for damages, repairs, and other lawful provisions of the lease or rental agreement.

The service member is required to give written notice of termination after entry on active duty or receipt of orders for active duty. The termination date for a lease/rental is 30 days after the first date on which the next rental payment is due after the termination notice is delivered. For example, if rent is due on the 1st of the month and notice is delivered to the landlord on August 5th, the next rent due is September 1st. Therefore, the lease/rental agreement will terminate on October 1st.

Reservists and members of the National Guard (when in active federal service) are also protected under the SSCRA.

Always work willingly with your military residents and be grateful for their service to our country.

Always work willingly with your military residents and be grateful for their service to our country.

Marketing for the next tenant

It is good practice to make sure your contracts give you, or your property management company, the right to begin marketing for a new tenant when the current one turns in notice. This allows you to put a sign in the yard and to begin showing the property immediately so that you might have a new tenant in place as soon as the old one vacates. Naturally, you'll give the current resident notice before bringing any prospects through.

Our experience, however, has been that properties often don't show well with tenants in them, especially with moving boxes and packing paper strewn everywhere. Because of this, we prefer to wait until the current tenant has moved completely before we begin showing the property. With our vacant properties, we know how they look and that they are move-in ready.

It won't take many rounds of replacing tenants before you discover which system works best for you.

Section Seven

ADDITIONAL

Chapter 24

PETS

Should you allow pets in your rental property?

Here are a couple of points to consider:

1. Millions of Americans own cats and dogs. Can you afford to miss out on this potential market?
2. Many people will tell you they have no pets. When you drive by the property, however, you may find otherwise.

Are you required to allow pets?

Are you required to allow pets? Absolutely not. The decision is up to you. However, note numbers one and two above.

As always, check applicable Fair Housing laws. Case in Point: We refused to allow pets in one home only to find out a prospective tenant had a service dog. By law, assistant (or service) animals must be allowed in any rental property, and you may not charge pet fees for

By law, assistant (or service) animals must be allowed in any rental property.

an assistant animal (service animals are not pets). Homeowners are responsible for damages the animal may cause and you may ask for proof that the animal is, in fact, a service animal.

Pet policy

No matter what your final pet policy, have it clearly spelled out in writing. We list our policy in both the rental application and the rental agreement. We do allow pets; however, we do have guidelines and we want there to be no question as to what our policy is.

For example, we allow no more than three pets. Take your pick: three dogs; three cats; two dogs and one cat; two cats and one dog—you get the idea.

We charge a nonrefundable pet deposit per pet.

We also charge a monthly rent per pet. Pets do damage, all of them, so we are very clear that they are allowed but there is a fee.

You may choose to enforce how many pets are allowed in each unit, size or weight limits, what types of animals, and which breeds. Some insurance companies refuse coverage for certain animals or breeds.

In addition, we attach a one page Pet Agreement to the lease. This document spells out that care, control, and all pet responsibilities belong to the tenant(s).

Be sure your rental agreement lists the names, descriptions, and weights of all pets you have cleared to live in the property.

Acquiring a pet later in the contract

Because so many people own pets, include a statement in your rental contract that, if a tenant acquires a pet after move-in, he or she must pay the pet deposit and begin pet rent at that time. Happily, tenants usually call to inform us when they are getting a pet.

If we discover a pet in the home, and that pet is not on the lease, the pet deposit and pet rent are due retroactively from the time of the lease signing (as spelled out in the rental contract). Amazingly, this has motivated confessions at the lease signing—confessions about the pet(s) they already have. More than one tenant has told me during our conversation at the contract signing, that they are temporarily keeping a pet for a family member. I tell them the nonrefundable pet deposit is due and they will be charged pet rent until the pet is returned to its owner. Not surprisingly, these pets continue to live in our property with the tenants.

People love their pets. Most are perfectly willing to pay the fees to have them in your property.

Most tenants will have pets, whether they want to admit it or not. Having this in-depth discussion up front allows you to collect the fees you will need to cover the repairs when they move out.

People love their pets. Most are perfectly willing to pay the fees to have them in your property.

Chapter 25

SHOULD YOU USE A PROPERTY MANAGEMENT COMPANY?

Property management can be a lot of work. Tenants don't need you only when it's convenient. Repairs and rent collections can wear down your spirits. Paying someone else to manage your properties may be worth every penny.

When purchasing your first property, you may believe handling a rental merely includes finding tenants, getting the lease signed, and receiving a check. Naturally, with some minor maintenance issues from time to time.

The reality is a bit more intense.

Property management

If you decide to rent out your property and manage it yourself, always handle your rental as a business, even if you have only one property. Do not become emotionally involved with your tenants (more easily said than done). Have rules and stick to them. If well managed, it will prosper. If poorly managed, it will fail.

If you decide to rent out your property and manage it yourself, always handle your rental as a business, even if you have only one property.

Should you decide to rent out your property but do not want to deal with tenants on your own, here are some things to consider when hiring a real estate or property management company:

- Most management companies won't attach the same importance to selecting good tenants and maintaining the property that you do.
- If you don't live nearby or don't want to manage for yourself, you need a good company with a good reputation to manage it for you.
- Interview multiple management companies—checking references and referrals—until you find one that you trust.
- Management fees will take part of your profits. In many cases, management and leasing fees can make the difference between positive cash flow (money left over after all expenses) and negative cash flow. Know your true numbers before making the decision.
- Have the management company you hire go over your numbers with you to give you a realistic idea of your costs and potential income.

What does a property management company do?

- Help you set accurate rental rates
- Make sure the property is compliant with state laws
- Market and advertise vacant properties
- Screen tenants
- Manage tenants
- Collect and deposit rents
- Handle repairs and tenant communications
- Provide vendors for service and repairs
- Renew rental agreements
- Handle all the time and legal hassle of evictions including going to court and meeting the sheriff for lock-outs
- Keep the books

Professional property management companies should have systems that allow them to manage all of the above efficiently. A good management company will work to prevent problems before they arise, as well as handle issues that come up in an effort to minimize any disruption to your income.

Most charge a small percentage of your monthly rent, what usually amounts to 10 percent, in exchange for their services. Compare that with the ten to fifteen hours per month you'd likely spend managing the property yourself, not to mention the mental anguish of being constantly on-call in case of emergency, and it may well be worth it to you.

We've heard from investors that, when owning rental properties as a full-time venture, twenty properties seems to be the tipping point. Most investors can manage properties on their own until twenty, then they're completely overwhelmed. At this point, they hire their own property manager or hand the properties over to a management company.

If you work full-time in another career, many factors will come up in deciding whether to manage on your own. Even if you start out managing your tenants in the beginning, it's nice to know that you have options. It's nice to know that you can own and profit from rental properties without handling all of the day-to-day landlording responsibilities yourself.

Chapter 26

TAX BENEFITS FOR LANDLORDS

The following is not meant to be a complete list, and I am not a tax consultant.

This chapter is to make you aware that there are tremendous tax benefits for owners of investment properties.

Before claiming any deductions, consult your tax advisor and/or CPA to find out which allowances work for you and anything additional you can use in the tax code to reduce your tax liability.

Before claiming any deductions, consult your tax advisor and/or CPA to find out which allowances work for you and anything additional you can use in the tax code to reduce your tax liability.

Partial list of tax benefits

- **Advertising costs**: As a landlord, you can take tax deductions for expenses related to filling vacancies.
- **Employee salaries and related expenses:** If you hire employees to help run your business, you can deduct their wages, social security contributions, health insurance premiums, and other expenses. This is also true when you hire an independent contractor (i.e., a repair person).
- **Home office:** There are of course guidelines, but you can deduct the expense of a business home office whether you own your home or are a renter.
- **Insurance premiums**: You can deduct your premiums for almost any insurance on your rental properties, including fire, theft, flood, and landlord liability. You can also deduct the cost of any employee insurance you provide.
- **Interest**: Just as with your personal residence, you can deduct interest paid on loans on your investment properties. You can also deduct credit card interest for purchases related to the upkeep and repair of your rental property.
- **Professional services**: As long as the fees and expenses are related to your rental properties, you can deduct legal expenses, accounting fees, broker commissions, property management company expenses, and other professional fees.
- **Property management fees:** If you use a property manager to maintain your rental properties and manage tenant relationships, his or her fees are fully tax deductible.
- **Property upkeep expenses**: Common expenses related to the upkeep of your income properties, such as trash removal, landscaping, HOA fees, and other maintenance costs, can be subtracted from your income.

- **Repairs**: Any expenses related to ordinary, necessary, and reasonable repairs (i.e., replacing a roof, fixing a leaky faucet) can be deducted from your tax bill. Unnecessary upgrades, however, are not considered "reasonable," so check with your CPA to be sure.
- **Self-employment expenses**: There are many additional tax deductions available to self-employed business owners, including phone, Internet, vehicle expenses related to business travel, and any business-related taxes you pay.
- **Travel:** For local travel, you can deduct your actual expenses (gasoline, upkeep, repairs) or you can use the standard mileage rate for your deduction (mileage rate changes annually). There are qualifications for mileage deductions, so find out what those are in your current tax year. For long-distance travel for your rental activity, you can deduct airfare, hotel bills, meals, and other expenses. Keep detailed records and properly document any travel expenses to avoid problems with the IRS.
- **Depreciation:** You can claim the depreciation of your rental property and the mechanical systems and appliances it contains as they age. This deduction is not taken all at once, but figured over time. The depreciation factor for single family residential property is 27.5 years, meaning you can take depreciation on the dwelling (not the land) spread out over 27.5 years.

You can claim the depreciation of your rental property and the mechanical systems and appliances it contains as they age.

How depreciation works

You buy a house for $100,000. The dwelling value is $80,000 and the land is $20,000. You cannot depreciate the land. Calculate depreciation on the dwelling by dividing its value by 27.5.

$80,000 ÷ 27.5 = $2,909.09

In this example, the depreciation allowance is $2,909 per year.

If you rent the property for $800 per month and your mortgage is $600 per month, you have a positive monthly cash flow of $200 or income of $2,400 per year.

Your income is now offset by the depreciation expense ($2,400 – $2,909 = -$509).

In this example, for tax purposes, you lost $509 on this property. This is a "paper loss" only, as you actually made $2,400.

So you received monthly cash flow, you're depreciating the property for tax write offs, and if you purchased correctly, you receive the added benefit of "appreciation" as the property value increases over time!

In our example, the depreciation put you at a paper loss even before deducting normal business expenses such as maintenance, cleaning, travel, supplies, interest, and taxes. The tax benefits when owning real estate go on and on!

You can further maximize the depreciation by doing what is known as "componentized," commonly known in accounting circles as "segregated," depreciation. This allows you to break out certain components of the property and depreciate them separately. For example, carpet, appliances, HVAC, and roof may be broken out and componentized as personal property, which can be depreciated even faster over only five years. Check

> *Landlording is a time-consuming, expensive, extremely detailed, highly regulated venture and you earn all the tax benefits you're allowed.*

with your CPA to see how you can implement componentization your business structure.

Landlording is a time-consuming, expensive, extremely detailed, highly regulated venture and you earn all the tax benefits you're allowed. There are so many tax benefits to landlording. Educate yourself on what the law allows you to claim and claim them.

For complete information on tax deductions for landlords, visit IRS Publication 527 at IRS.gov.

Chapter 27

RISKS OF LEAVING YOUR PROPERTY VACANT

Do you have a vacant property? Has it been vacant for more than thirty days? If so, you may not have insurance coverage. Most landlords continue to pay their premium but, if a claim is filed, it may not be paid because vacancy can void the policy.

A property that has been vacant more than thirty days may not be covered on your landlord insurance policy.

A property that has been vacant more than thirty days may not be covered on your landlord insurance policy.

Vacancy insurance

Some insurance companies cover vacant properties through landlord policies for up to ninety days. If you have a vacant property, you must have vacancy insurance.

Vacant house insurance can be more expensive than regular landlord insurance, often double, for a number of obvious reasons:

- There's no one living in the house to watch and protect it
- Vacant properties tend to be a target for thieves, vandals, and vagrants
- The potential for water damage and infestations of animals or insects goes up

Insurance companies put a high risk (and cost) on insuring vacant properties because of the increased risk of theft, vandalism, fire, water, and pest damage. These risks and costs may be higher in Northern states because of potential damage due to extreme weather (frozen pipes bursting, etc.).

Talk with your agent about vacancy coverage and rates.

Some suggestions about vacant property

Protect your property. Install and use a monitored security system and make sure the smoke detectors are functioning. If your property has a sprinkler system, monitored central alarm for fire, smoke and theft detectors, and deadbolt locks, your home is safer and these features may lower your insurance premiums.

Make the house look lived in. Ask a neighbor to keep an eye on the house and park a car in your driveway. Install timers on lights and leave window coverings and some furniture in the home. Keep the home maintained by mowing the yard, cleaning gutters, trimming trees, checking for leaks, shoveling the sidewalks and driveway, and winterizing or maintaining as necessary.

Keeping your property secure

Every fourteen seconds, a home is robbed. Most robberies happen during the day. According to statistics by the Federal Bureau of Investigation, the average dollar loss per burglary is over $2,000.

With the national economy struggling, burglary is a more common crime. But, it doesn't take much to get the thieves to leave your house alone. What can you do to keep your personal home as well as your rental property secure?

1. **Have a secure front door.** The front door is the No. 1 point of entry for thieves. Most of the time, intruders knock to see if anyone's there, then just stand back and kick in the front door. Make sure it's an exterior door, different than what you'd use for the bedroom. Make sure it's solid core construction or metal clad. And make sure it's secured by three-inch screws rather than the typical one-inch screws so it's secured to the structure, rather than just the doorframe.

The front door is the No. 1 point of entry for thieves.

2. **Peep hole**. Have a peephole in your door so it doesn't have to be opened to see who's there. The best ones are wide-angle viewers.

3. **Exterior doors.** Sixty percent of all burglaries take place at ground floor doors and windows. All entry doors should be solid wood or steel-wrapped wood-core doors.

4. **Garage doors and windows** should be treated as any exterior door and window. Keep them closed and locked. Burglars can enter through your garage undetected from the outside. Once inside the garage, a burglar can use your tools to break into your home, out of sight of the neighbors.

5. **Porch and patio doors.** Take extra precaution with porch and patio doors because these doors are less observable from the street and by neighbors.

6. **Locks.** Key-in-the-knob locks can be forced quickly and without much effort. If you have this type of lock, be sure to add a dead bolt. And not all dead bolts are the same. Research to get one that will truly secure your door. Be sure to attach the dead bolt with three-inch screws that penetrate through the frame to the structure. If you have glass within forty inches of the dead bolt, it is recommended that you use a dead bolt lock that is key operated from both inside and out. Don't leave the key sitting in the inside lock or, by simply breaking the glass, someone can reach in and unlock the door!

7. **Windows**. All ground-floor windows should be closed and locked when you're away. Keep bushes and shrubs trimmed back so your windows are not hidden, which would give privacy to intruders. And make sure all tree branches are cut back from upper-level windows to prevent access. Close and lock upper floor windows when you are away.

8. **Basement Windows.** Keep basement windows closed and locked. If not used, secure permanently with nails that extend into the structure.

9. **Lock windows and doors.** Having secure doors and windows is not enough; they must be locked! I was surprised to read that many people don't bother. Of all reported burglaries, 33.2 percent were unlawful entries (without force)—meaning the house wasn't even locked.

10. **Close shades and curtains in the evening.** One way thieves decide where to strike is simply by window-shopping. Close the blinds so they won't see inside.

11. **Spare Keys.** Don't hide spare keys. Burglars know about fake rocks and statues and will check under doormats, in

mailboxes, and over doorways. Make sure everyone in the family has a spare key and give a spare set to a neighbor.

12. **Ladders.** Don't store ladders outdoors or in unlocked sheds. These can be used to reach the roof and upper floor windows.

13. **Silent alarms.** We all hate noisy alarms, so do burglars. Thieves know it can take ten to twenty minutes for the alarm company or police to show up after an alarm has been tripped. It's best to have both silent and audible alarms.

14. **Landscaping.** Tall hedges and shrubs near the house create hiding spots. Keep doorways, porches and windows clear. Overhanging branches can be a way to access upper decks or your roof.

15. **Lawn Care**. A well-manicured lawn indicates someone is home. Be sure to have your lawn cared for even when you are on vacation or the property is vacant.

16. **Exterior lighting.** All exterior entrances should be well lighted. Poor or absent exterior lighting allows dark and shadows where burglars can work unobserved. Many can be controlled to go on and off depending upon daylight and motion sensors go on automatically in response to motion. This sudden light not only scares away intruders but alerts you and your neighbors as well.

17. **Indoor timers.** When you are away from home, leave a few lights on. Use timers to turn lights on and off at normal times. You can even set TVs or radios to turn on and off. Set timers to go on thirty minutes before dark so it looks like someone is in the house. While on vacation, have them go off at random times when you'd normally go to bed.

18. **Sliding glass doors**. Most sliding glass doors are easy to jiggle free of locks and slide open easily. An inexpensive security measure is to place a dowel in the channel so the door can't be pried open. Sliding doors are lifted into

position when installed and can be lifted from the track to be removed by a burglar. Insert two or three sheet metal screws into the track above the door to prevent this. Adjust the screws so the top of the door barely clears them when opened or closed. Lock the door with a dead bolt.

19. **Install deadbolts**, especially on a door with a glass section or located near a window. With a deadbolt, if the glass is broken and someone tries to reach in to open the door, they won't be able to. There are two main types of deadbolts: single and double cylinder locks. A single cylinder deadbolt has a keyed opening on one side and a knob that can be turned by hand on the other. A double cylinder deadbolt lock is keyed on both sides. Determine which you prefer for your particular need.

20. **Don't rely on your barking dog.** Serious burglars know dogs may back away from someone wielding a weapon, or get chummy if offered a treat laced with a tranquilizer. Better to make your home look occupied with timers that turn electronics on and off in random patterns.

21. **Watch what you throw out.** Don't advertise your brand new flat-screen TV, appliances, or other big-ticket item by putting boxes at the curb with your trash. Break down boxes into small pieces and bundle them so you can't tell what was inside.

22. **Social media.** Never post vacation info on Facebook or any other social media sites. Burglars troll social media sites looking for targets. Wait until you get back before sharing vacation details.

23. **GPS**. NEVER use your home address in your GPS. Thieves break into cars, and then steal the GPS and garage door opener. Now they know where you live and have the ability to break in. Instead use a location, preferably a business, nearby as your home location.

24. **Mail, Newspapers and FedEx.** When you are out of town, be sure to stop your mail, newspapers, and any other scheduled deliveries. At the very least, have a neighbor pick them up for you daily. Nothing says, "we're not here" like deliveries piling up at your home.

25. **Don't hesitate** to report suspicious activities in your neighborhood. I once had two men knock on my door. One was holding a clipboard. They claimed to be from the local electric company and said they needed to see my last three electric bills. I said that I didn't have them, that they'd need to send the request by mail, and I shut the door. I immediately called the electric company. Of course, the electric company would never do such a thing, so I phoned the police and every neighbor whose phone number I had.

Which brings me to the final suggestion.

26. **Neighborhood Watch Program** - How about forming a Neighborhood Watch Program in your neighborhood? Neighbors learn how to secure their homes, agree to report suspicious activities on their block, have a communication network established, and put out signs to alert intruders driving through the area. Again, anyone interested in committing a crime will move on to another area.

Simply make forced entry difficult or risky and any burglar will move onto another property.

It's easy and inexpensive to minimize your chance of being a target. Simply make forced entry difficult or risky and any burglar will move onto another property. Your local law enforcement will be happy to advise and assist you and your neighbors.

Crime prevention begins at home!

Words from Other Landlords

We have been coaching and training others in our area to invest in real estate for years. Many of them now own their own rental properties and have become landlords in the process. I asked them to allow me to include some of their stories here for your benefit.

Landlords have some amazing tales to tell!

What I have learned to date on landlording

"We will not put you out of your house; you will put you out of your house by not paying the rent as stated in your signed contract."

1. You cannot make a tenant your friend. (My nature tends to lean this way.) The relationship between you and the tenant is business and cannot be made personal. If there is an emotional relationship, then unmet expectations by either the tenant or the landlord will cause problems.

2. In communicating with a tenant, I use several illustrations or phrases that keep the compassion in my answer but maintain a business relationship. When they plead, "Please do not put me out," I turn the responsibility back to them by responding, "We will not put you out of your house; **you** will put **you** out of your house by not paying the rent as stated in your signed contract." Another point I use in conversation to infer validation to the tenant and take away the bad guy image is, "This is not about you and me, Mrs. Smith. You and I could be friends, BUT you and Green Tree Properties have a **contract** and that is what I need to uphold."

3. I have to remind myself it's not personal. Again my nature says, "If they like me, they will be nice to me, keep the property in good shape, pay on time, and not lie." I know this is false but, again, it is where my nature takes me (back to that friendship thing).

4. Do not make the company "you work for" look too bad. If you make the company the enemy, it is bad for business. You never want to act like you are on the tenant's side at the expense of the company just to get a desired result. They could spray paint the walls before they leave. "Terry was really nice to us but you are a mean company." Deflecting responsibility back to the company needs to be handled wisely.

5. Compliment tenants in areas where they excel if you see one. If they pay on time, let them know you recognize that. If the house is spotless and clean each time you go into it, compliment and thank them. If they make repairs or take the initiative to fix something without calling you, let them know you appreciate what they have done. We all grew up in a system that rewards good behavior. It still counts. We all like to get a gold star on our chart. A small gift at an appropriate time to say thank you is smart business. It will also reinforce the good behavior.

6. You have an application for a reason. Use it. If there are blanks on the page, the house stays empty.

So far, this is what I have experienced (or learned the hard way).

Terry Parker, Green Tree Properties

My worst horror story

It's my worst horror story but, compared to some, it's not that bad.

It was a lease option sale, supposedly. But the tenant/buyers I put in there were never going to get a loan. I was desperate to fill the property because I had relied on someone else to find me a lease option buyer (a supposed expert in our local area). I thought he was the expert in everything real estate. And I needed some help because my financial situation was rough at the time. We had just had our third child and I had lost my job the month before.

I finally got a couple with one child and one on the way in the house. WHEW! I thought: disaster avoided. Well, right after they moved in, they wanted to "fix" the house up a bit. Since they were going to be the future owners of the house, I thought, why not. The husband worked in the home improvement industry and he could do most of the work himself. It was an older house, and it did suffer from some functional obsolescence. We wrote out a scope of work agreement. They started doing the work. In the third month, the rent was late. The fourth month's rent didn't come at all. After repeated attempts to get in contact with them, they told me that the hubbie's job had cut his hours. The wife was about to give birth so I don't think she was working at the time.

They paid one month's rent, but the next was late, so on and so on, for seven or eight months. At this point, they were about three full months behind and not returning my calls or letters. Before I evicted them (it was my first eviction), I thought I'd go by there one last time to make contact in person. One other thing I had done to try to help the family out was to have the electricity in my name and the house was heated with a heat pump. So, my wife and I go over there about 8:30 one chilly February night. The house was completely dark. Even though it was winter, the grass was high and unkempt. I'm asking myself if they still lived there. I knocked but got no answer. So, I proceeded to enter the premises. As soon as I opened the door I was immediately hit with a blast of hot air. No, it wasn't on fire. The thermostat was set to 90 degrees! And they're not even there!

I talked to the neighbor, and she said they hadn't been there all day. That was the last straw. I filed the eviction papers the next Monday morning.

The worst part was that I hadn't seen their most recent "upgrades" to the house. It came as quite a shock. They had torn down a wall between the living room and a hallway, but hadn't finished their project. The work they had done wasn't that bad actually. It's just that I was now going to have to add in fix-up costs to this fiasco.

They actually moved out the weekend after the eviction and, after talking with them, I decided not to pursue a judgment. All in all, I believe we lost about $5,000 on that deal. I ended up selling it for just above the loan balance. Just enough extra to cover the closing costs. It still needed a little bit of work to finish it up, and I was just glad to be done with it.

As you can tell, I made a bunch of mistakes. Live and learn. Gotta love the School of Hard Knocks.

Paul Holt, Results Home Solutions

How I Avoid Bad Tenants

1. We use a "security deposit addendum," which clarifies exactly under what conditions the tenant can expect to receive a full refund of the security deposit. Otherwise, the general wording in the standard lease agreement allows the property to be returned in a manner consistent with "reasonable wear and tear" (whatever that means). We also do a HD DVD recording of the condition of the property at move-in and deliver this recording plus the standard paper move-in inspection report to the tenant. The tenant then has ten days to make corrections to the report. If no corrections are made, the tenant is accepting the property in the condition we have reported. On average, we have been keeping $500 in deposits to cover items noted in the addendum. This applies to deposits where deductions have been necessary. In most cases, properties have been returned in PERFECT condition and we gladly refund the full deposit.

2. Video. Here is the hot link (How do I Avoid Bad Tenants). We offer a free report for property management customers. Since the video is on the website, any tenant can see the video, which sends a signal that we intend to thoroughly screen tenants. By the way, we have had no evictions and

only a few late payments since we started Paramount Realty fourteen months ago.

3. We conduct interior property inspections, conducted at around the ninety-day point of occupancy. We send our handyman out to look at the outside and inside of the property. We have found extra people (charged more rent), extra animals (charged more deposits), early signs of animal damage (made the Tenant repair immediately and we agreed to let her go from the property after only 90 days of renting--- under the condition that she repaired the damage and kept the property show ready). We lost no time for the Owner and let the Tenant go without penalty. The whole process cost the Owner zero dollars.

Fred Fetterolf, ParamountRealtySolutions.com

Never wait to file eviction

We had a Section 8, government-subsidized tenant—let's call her Ms. White. Well, Ms. White could not afford to pay, so we filed eviction.

On the day we did the lockout, she had done nothing to prepare to move. She begged us not to kick her out and asked if she could pay me really fast so I would not evict her. I told her, "yes." She called her whole family and raised the $380.00 she owed us so we decided not to remove her. I felt sorry for her, which was my first mistake.

Two months later she was behind again, so we filed eviction again. On the second lockout date, I was standing outside in the rain with the local sheriff getting ready to change the locks when Ms. White walked out in her PJs. We promptly told her it was time to leave and she said nobody had told her this was going to happen, and could she please have more time. The sheriff reminded her that it was posted on her front door so she knew and she needed to get out now.

The only reason Ms. White had to pay the rent was because her adult son would not move out. He also failed to help out with the rent and was asleep upstairs in his room at 11a.m., hung-over from drinking the previous night.

Ms. White had not packed anything. She mistakenly assumed I would feel sorry for her again and let her stay. She was wrong. So we changed the locks and kicked her and her son out of the house. They had to sit on the front porch waiting for a ride in the rain. I had my 10- and 12-year-old boys in the car waiting on me, so this was a good life lesson for them.

We posted the home, changed the locks, and left. I waited until ten days had passed, expecting the tenant to call us and make an appointment to come get her stuff. She never did. We assumed she broke back in and just took all her stuff out. On day eleven after the lockout, William, my 10-year-old, and I went to inspect the house and make sure all the food was out. (Never leave food to rot in one of your rentals; you will be sorry. I won't tell you how I learned that.)

Much to my surprise, all of her stuff was still there and the electricity was still on. I said to my son, "It's almost as if she's still living here." I figured there was no way she would be that dumb. So William and I spent the next hour and a half removing bag after bag after bag of empty liquor and beer bottles, over nine bags worth, and about five bags of food and trash from the kitchen. There was more than $1,000 worth of alcohol consumed in that unit. Now we knew why the rent wasn't being paid. We also found a bag of marijuana (which we got rid of) and four electric meter tags in the cabinets of the kitchen. I looked out back at my meter only to discover they had torn off the meter cover and installed a stolen meter. We called the power company and found out there had not been legal power on in the unit for five months.

While we were cleaning, I thought I heard a noise upstairs but I said to myself, "Must have been one of the neighbors." So we decided to go through the rest of the house to see what cool stuff she had left for us, since we now owned all the contents of the house.

We walked the entire house and noticed she had left everything behind, even her purse. We were shocked. At that point, I looked all over the house and found no one. So we began to take out the less-than-a-year-old 32" flat-screen TV, the new-looking electric guitar and amp, the iPod, more than 160 new DVDs, a 1923 $20 dollar bill, a huge bowl of change with $40 in it, a Sony Play Station 3 with about fifteen games, and a few other cool things. We set those items in my van and decided to videotape the condition of the home and the items we removed because I had never, in my nine years of doing this, had this happen before.

Now, the whole time we are doing this, I was explaining to my son how he needed to do his homework and get good grades in school and work hard so that he would never end up like Ms. White.

We had documented the entire house and were filming in the master bedroom when out from the closet popped Ms. White, which freaked me out. I asked her what was she doing in my house and told her she needed to get out - now! She admitted (on video) that she had broken back into the home because she had nowhere else to stay. I told her to get what she could get into her purse and get out, Now!

Ms. White asked if she could have more time to get her stuff. At this point, I was angry because she and broken and entered the house, stolen power, ripped me off, and lied to everyone. I told her again to get out immediately and called the police. I told them not to arrest her, to just remove her and tell her to never come back or the next time I would have her arrested.

I was very thankful to have it all on tape. My son William learned the value of being honest and working hard and was rewarded with an electric guitar and amp that he is now learning to play. In the end, I got some cash, a new TV, and some videos, so all was not lost.

Never wait to file eviction. Always file as soon as you can. Have no mercy on the dead beats who are stealing from you. Kick them out fast. It is business. Always be polite, but be firm. Hopefully you will not have the same troubles I did.

Bill Sanford, Advantage Homebuyers

A Bit About Late Fees

I want to say a bit about late fees.

1. You have to charge them or a lot of people would never worry about the due date.

2. Even when you charge them, a lot of people still don't pay much attention.

What amazes me is the number of people who pay late, including the late fees, every single month. If we were to raise their rent to the amount they pay every month with the extra 5%, I'm sure they would move. However, they don't mind paying the fees every single month rather than simply paying on the date they're due.

And, contrary to what tenants believe, we don't want to collect late fees! We want them to pay on-time so we don't have to chase them, can clear off our books, and can move onto other things we need to get done.

If you're a landlord, don't worry about charging late fees because 1. you earn them and, 2. late paying tenants don't appear to mind paying them anyway!

Veronica Serna, Triad Residential Solutions

Thanks to all the landlords who shared their stories here. As you can see, landlording is quite a varied experience.

I hope you'll join us in this exciting, profitable venture of creating safe, affordable housing for others.

To your success!

Epilogue

I have been investing in real estate since 2004, and I now do coaching and training for real estate investors (check out our website: www.TriadMastermind.com). I also own a full service real estate and property management company www.AllPropertySolutions.com. I write real estate articles for my blog four to five times per week at www.KarensPerspective.com, and I write books.

What I've found when helping buyers, sellers, landlords, and investors is that many of you prefer to hold the printed word rather than reading articles or a blog online. You want to mark it up, make notes in the margin, and tag pages for reference.

For you, I've put together these books so you have all the information you need in one spot to carry with you and reference with ease.

Many thanks to you for your interest, and if you are left with unanswered questions or have a real estate story or success you'd like to share, please contact me through my blog www.KarensPerspective.com, or e-mail me directly at karen@karensperspective.com.

I look forward to hearing from you, and may you have tremendous real estate success!

About the Author

Karen Rittenhouse is a full-time real estate investor. She's been involved in real estate since 2000, when she purchased her first investment property, and full time since January 2005. In the past few years, Karen has bought and sold more than 150 single-family homes. She is not a real estate agent. All of the deals with which she's been involved have been her own.

Karen also does local coaching and training, and has found through her travels nationally that many people recognize the value of investing in real estate—some with only their personal homes, others as a way to produce present and future income. Most people simply don't know how to get started, what to do next, or where to get information. That's the purpose of her writing—concise, abundant information.

Before turning to real estate, Karen sold high-end furniture and did interior design. So, as you can see, much of her working career has been involved with creating nurturing home environments. Her goal here is to help people who want to realize the dream of creating long-term wealth through owning and holding real estate.

Terms & Definitions

Many of these words are used throughout this book. I thought it would be easier for you if they were listed alphabetically here. They aren't all official definitions; many are friendly explanations as I would explain them in person. For more real estate definitions, check out one of my favorite sites, Investopedia.com.

Automated Clearing House (ACH)—An electronic funds-transfer system run by the National Automated Clearing House Association to facilitate electronic transfers of money.

Bank Check—Purchased at the bank with cash, also known as a cashier's check, demand draft, or teller's check—bank checks are treated as guaranteed funds by the issuing bank (because you purchased them with cash!).

Closing—This is when ownership of the property is transferred from seller to buyer. At this time, all documents are signed and recorded.

Comp—In real estate, comp is short for comparable sale. These are sales of similar homes in the same or similar neighborhoods as the property you are evaluating. By comparing similar characteristics between homes of comparable size, value, and age, buyers are better able to determine the true property value of the home they want to purchase.

Compliant—Conforms to requirements.

Componentized or Segregated Depreciation—Breaking down a large purchase, repair, or renovation expenditure into a number of smaller repair categories. This allows accelerated tax depreciation of certain items like roofs and appliances.

Constructive Notice—Signifies that a person is legally presumed to have knowledge of something, even if they have no actual knowledge of it.

CPA—Certified Public Accountant

Credit Score—A numeric expression of creditworthiness ranging from 350 to 800.

Default—Failure to make a payment when due.

Depreciation—For accounting purposes, depreciation indicates how much of an asset's value has been used up. As an example, for your rental properties, your CPA can depreciate the value of your roof as it ages, giving you some tax advantage.

Electronic Fund Transfer (EFT)—The electronic exchange or transfer of money from one account to another. For landlords, this allows auto payments from the tenant's bank account into yours.

Equity—The difference between what is owed on the mortgage and what the property is worth.

Escrow—Monies held by a third party on behalf of lender and borrower. When all agreement conditions are met, the money held in escrow transfers to the appropriate entities.

Fair Market Value—The price a given property would sell for.

Fixed Interest Rate—An interest rate that will not change.

Fixed Rate Mortgage—A loan or mortgage that will remain at a constant rate for the entire term of the loan.

Foreclosure—Termination of the mortgage rights of the homeowner. When a lender takes possession of a mortgaged property because someone failed to make mortgage payments.

HOA—Homeowners Association—An organization that assists with maintaining and improving groups of property.

HOA Fees or Dues—Money paid monthly by owners of residential property to the Homeowners Association. Assists with maintaining and improving that property.

Lessee—The person or entity leasing the property as a tenant.

Lease with Option to Buy or **Lease-to-Own**—Similar to a rental except that the lessee/tenant is actually working toward owning that home at a future date.

Lease Option Fee—Or "down payment" to move into a lease-to-own property. This buys the lessee the right to purchase the home at a future date and locks in the purchase price.

Market Value—The price for which a given property would sell.

MLS—Multiple Listing Service, where real estate agents publish their property listings.

Mortgage Insurance—An insurance policy to compensate lenders or investors for losses due to the default of a mortgage loan.

Professional Real Estate Status—An IRS classification. For the IRS to classify you with Real Estate Professional status, you must work in the business 750 hours per year and more than half of your working hours must be in real estate.

Promissory Note—A written, dated, and signed two-party contract containing conditions by which the maker will pay a definite sum of money to a payee on demand or at a specified future date.

Property Insurance—Provides protection against most risks to the property such as fire, theft, and some weather damage.

PITI—Principle, Interest, Taxes, and Insurance, often all rolled together into your monthly mortgage payment.

Rent Premium—When a tenant is in a property on a lease to buy option, in addition to the normal rent, he or she pays an additional fee, known as the rent premium. Accrued rent premiums are subtracted from the purchase price of the house if the renter exercises the option to buy. If there is no eventual purchase, the seller of the house gets to keep this extra premium.

Service Animals—Animals trained to perform tasks that assist people with disabilities.

Section 8 Housing—Government-subsidized housing program that helps lower income families afford rent by paying a portion of the market price for rental units. Funded by the Department of Housing and Urban Development.

Seller Financing—A loan offered by the seller to the buyer of the property. This can make selling easier as the buyer does not have to obtain a bank loan.

Sub-lease—When the original tenant, who has leased the premises from the owner, leases out all or a portion of the premises to a new tenant

Tax Credit—Dollar for dollar reduction in tax owed. For example, you owe $28,000 in taxes. You have a $2,000 tax credit. You take $2,000 off the total amount you owe, so you now owe only $26,000.

Tax Deduction—Amount you subtract from your gross income to figure out how much of your income is taxable. For example, your gross income is $100,000 and you have a $2,000 tax deduction. You subtract $2,000 from your taxable income which is now only $98,000.

Internet Resource Links

Calculators

- **Mortgage Calculator**
  mortgageloan.com/calculator/

Crime Check

- CrimeReports.com
- Crimemapping.com
- Spotcrime.com

Free Sites to List Properties

- **Trulia**
  trulia.com
- **Zillow**
  zillow.com
- **Craigslist**
  craigslist.org
- **Postlets**
  www.postlets.com

Landlord / Tenant Laws

- **Laws & Statutes by State**
  www.uslandlord.com/laws/

- **Landlord Protection Agency—Rental forms, tenant law info**
  http://bit.ly/QxıdaC
- **HUD Housing Choice Vouchers—Section 8 information**
  http://bit.ly/hudhousing
- **National Fair Housing Alliance**
  http://www.nationalfairhousing.org/
- RentLaw.com
  National Landlord Tenant Laws
- **National Low Income Housing Coalition**
  http://nlihc.org/
- NOLO.com
  Law center for landlords and tenants

Maps

- **Bing**
  Bing.com/maps
- **Yahoo**
  maps.yahoo.com
- **Google**
  maps.google.com

Online Rent Payment Tools

- ClearNow.com
- eRentPayment.com
- PayClix.com
- PayLease.com
- PayYourRent.com
- RAMSRent.com
- RentMatic.com

- SmartRentOnline

Rental Amounts

- RentRange.com
- Rento-o-Meter.com

Tax Deductions

- FindLaw.com
- RentLaw.com
- **Rental Property Tax Deductions**
  http://bit.ly/Oub4ht

Tenant Screening

- **ATenantScreen.com**
  http://www.atenantscreen.com/
- eRenter.com
- **Experian**
  http://ex.pn/PWxIlr
- **National Tenant Network**
  http://www.ntnonline.com/
- **TRexGlobal**
  http://bit.ly/N41G2L

Additional

- **Americans with Disabilities Act**
  http://1.usa.gov/ADAct
- **Fair Housing Act**
  http://bit.ly/FairHousingAdvocate
- **Housing Predictor—forecasts for all 50 states**
  housingpredictor.com/

- **Lead Based Paint Laws**
  http://www.epa.gov/lead/pubs/regulation.htm
- **National Association of Realtors® website**
  http://www.realtor.org/
- **Real Estate Definitions**
  Investopedia.com
- **Federal Consumer Protection Agency**
  ftc.gov/
- **Home Inspectors Directory Inspection checklist**
  tinyurl.com/inspectionlist

Important PDFs

- **Fair Credit Reporting Act**
  http://bit.ly/faircreditreportingact
- **FTC Red Flags Rule**
  http://bit.ly/FTCredflagsrule
- **Service Members Civil Relief Act (SCRA)**
  http://bit.ly/servicememberscivilrelief
- **Renters Rights in Foreclosure Laws**
  http://bit.ly/rentersrightsinforeclosurelaws
- **Federal Fair Housing Act**
  http://bit.ly/FederalFairHousingAct

Index

F

G

H

I

K

L

M

N

O

P

R

Be Sure to Check Out Karen's Other Books

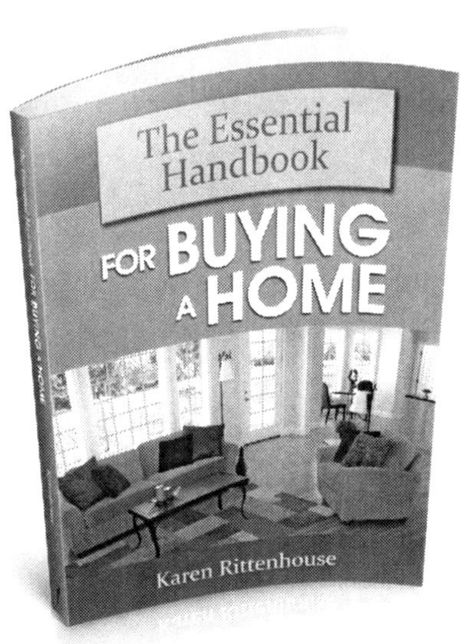

Look for Karen's companion books at KarensPerspective.com, Amazon.com or wherever fine books are sold!

For more free real estate information and training, scan this code or go to KarenRittenhouseBook.com